Hiking the Black Hills Country

Help Us Keep This Guide Up to Date

Every effort has been made by the authors and editors to make this guide as accurate and use-ful as possible. However, many things can change after a guide is published—trails are rerouted, regulations change, techniques evolve, facilities come under new management, etc.

We would love to hear from you concerning your experiences with this guide and how you feel it could be improved and kept up to date. While we may not be able to respond to all comments and suggestions, we'll take them to heart, and we'll also make certain to share them with the authors. Please send your comments and suggestions to the following address:

> The Globe Pequot Press
> Reader Response/Editorial Department
> P.O. Box 480
> Guilford, CT 06437

Or you may e-mail us at:

> editorial@GlobePequot.com

Thanks for your input, and happy trails!

A FALCON GUIDE®

Hiking the Black Hills Country

Country

A Guide to More Than 50 Hikes in South Dakota and Wyoming

Second Edition

Bert and Jane Gildart

FALCON GUIDE®

GUILFORD, CONNECTICUT
HELENA, MONTANA
AN IMPRINT OF THE GLOBE PEQUOT PRESS

Published in partnership with the Black Hills Parks and Forest Association.

Text design by Nancy Freeborn
All interior photographs by Bert and Jane Gildart
Maps by David Sami, Multi Mapping LTD., M.A.Dubé © Morris Book Publishing, LLC

Gildart, Robert, C.
  Hiking the Black Hills country / Bert and Jane Gildart. — 2nd ed.
        p. cm. — (A Falcon guide)
    ISBN 0-7627-3547-3
    1. Hiking—South Dakota—Guidebooks. 2. Hiking—Black Hills (S.D. and Wyo.)—Guidebooks. 3. South Dakota—Guidebooks. 4. Black Hills (S.D. and Wyo.)—Guidebooks. I. Gildart, Jane. II. Title. III. Series

  GV199.42.S6G55 2005
  917.83'90434—dc22   2005050227

Manufactured in the United States of America
Second Edition/First Printing

To Scott, Karen, Angie, Katie, and David.
May the mountains, prairies, and trails always beckon you.

Contents

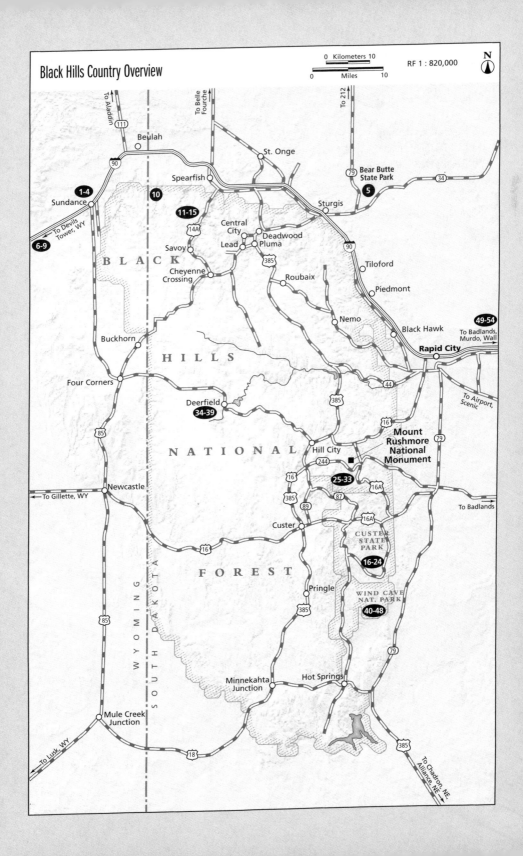

Black Hills Country Overview

Kilometers 10

Miles 10

RF 1 : 820,000

N

To Aladdin

111

Beulah

To Belle Fourche

To 212

90

1-4

Sundance

10

Spearfish

St. Onge

79

Bear Butte State Park

34

5

To Devils Tower, WY

6-9

11-15

14A

Central City

Sturgis

90

Savoy

Lead

Deadwood Pluma

385

Tiloford

49-54

Cheyenne Crossing

Roubaix

Piedmont

To Badlands, Murdo, Wall

B L A C K

Nemo

Black Hawk

Buckhorn

H I L L S

Rapid City

Four Corners

44

To Airport, Scenic

Deerfield

385

34-39

16

To Badlands

85

N A T I O N A L

Hill City

79

244

Mount Rushmore National Monument

16

25-33

16A

Newcastle

385

87

89

To Gillette, WY

Custer

16A

To Badlands

16

CUSTER STATE PARK

F O R E S T

16-24

Pringle

WIND CAVE NAT. PARK

385

40-48

85

W Y O M I N G

S O U T H   D A K O T A

79

Minnekahta Junction

Hot Springs

Mule Creek Junction

To Lusk, WY

18

385

To Chadron, NE; Alliance, NE

Acknowledgments

No book ever gets into print without lots of help. This one is no exception. During the course of our work, we have relied on many people, particularly those associated with the various management agencies of the Black Hills.

From our readers we learned much and, although the list is long, we'd like to mention the following people, who helped us immeasurably: Jerry Hagen, trail coordinator for the Bearlodge District in Wyoming; Jim Jandreau, park manager of Bear Butte State Park; Christine Czazasty, chief of interpretation at Devils Tower National Monument; Marianne Mills, chief of resource education of Badlands National Park; Craig Pugsley, visitor services coordinator of Custer State Park; Ron Walker, Custer State Park; Tom Farrell, chief of interpretation at Wind Cave National Park; Phyllis Cremonini, assistant chief of interpretation at Wind Cave National Park; Scott E. Spleiss, in the Deerfield area; Steve Baldwin, executive director of the Black Hills Parks & Forests Association for his fact-checking and for supplying the GPS coordinates; Galen Roesler, in the Spearfish area; Loren Poppert and Rusty Wilder in the Harney Range area; Laura Burns from the USDA Forest Service, Hell Canyon Ranger District; Gus Malon, Forest Service wilderness technician; and the USDA Forest Service for maps of the Harney area. Much appreciation is given also to the many good and talented folks at The Globe Pequot Press who were involved in the creation of this book, especially assistant editor Julie Marsh.

We also would like to thank fellow FalconGuide writers Will Harmon and Donald W. Pfitzer for use of regional material and information about hiking with children. Last, but never least, many kudos to our editor Bill Schneider for his guidance and patience. If we have forgotten anyone, we apologize.

Introduction

The Black Hills are a hiker's delight. Contained in these 6,000 square miles of un-glaciated valleys and hills are more than 500 miles of trails that do great things. For one, they take you to splendid fishing. For another, they weave among incredible scenery sculpted by time in accordance with some of the nation's most provocative geological mandates. What all this results in is variety—something for everyone.

This fact is more readily appreciated once you begin to envision the area's im-mensity and the way in which it has affected travelers through the ages—including Crazy Horse, George Armstrong Custer, and a man named Colonel Dodge, who upon approaching the Black Hills wrote, "The Black Hills country is a true oasis in a wide and dreary desert."

Just what is this Black Hills Country? We think it's a hiker's paradise. The hills' name was ascribed to them by the native people who first lived here and who called them the Paha Sapa, meaning "hills that are black." The hills appear that way due to the predominance of ponderosa pines. The interplay of light and sun influence the overall effect of blackness produced by these trees.

Geologically, the land represents the easternmost extension of the Rocky Moun-tain uplift, which covers an elliptical expanse of nearly 6,000 square miles. The Black Hills themselves extend about 120 miles north to south and about 40 to 50 miles east to west. At an elevation of 7,242 feet, Harney Peak is the region's highest moun-tain. This peak is contained in what geologists refer to as the Central Area. Sur-rounding it are three rimlike features known as the Limestone Plateau, the Red Valley, and the Hogback Ridge. For ease of visualization, geologists suggest you pic-ture these features in the form of a bird's nest ringing Harney Peak.

Outside the "nest" are other areas that provide great trekking. For the purposes of this guide, we've included the Badlands as well as Devils Tower and the Bearlodge Mountains in Wyoming, which were created by the same forces as the Black Hills. Although divided politically, these areas are contiguous geologically, and we discuss them together here.

With such diverse terrain, there's little wonder some of the region's trails, such as the Centennial and the George S. Mickelson Trail, extend for more than a hundred miles, while others extend but for a few. We've included a wide range of trails. It's up to you to decide which of the many routes described herein you'd like to hike.

Getting There

In South Dakota, take Interstate 90 (I–90) from the east or west; U.S. Highway 385, 85, or 79 from the north or south; or U.S. Highway 16 or 34 from the east or west to the Black Hills and enter from any number of signposted locations.

How to Use This Guide

More than fifty trails wander through the Black Hills, logging 500-plus miles. For hikers faced with this vast country, knowing where to start can be difficult. This guide provides the basic kind of information that will help hikers select trails according to their abilities and interests. We've hiked all the trails on public land in Black Hills Country. Here we give brief descriptions of each geographic region and its primary routes.

The book is divided into sections, one for each of the major geographic regions. Each of these sections begins with an overview, in which we describe the reasons a person would want to hike a trail in that particular area. The aesthetics of the Black Hills' incredible natural history as well as the history of those who have preceded us here through the ages often provide compelling reasons to wander. The overview also offers tips intended to facilitate your outing, something even veteran hikers might appreciate.

Following the overview are hike descriptions for each main trail we cover, beginning with an outline describing the physical characteristics of the trail for quick and easy reference. We've also provided "hike specs" that include all of the statistical information you might need for that particular hike. You'll notice that each entry has a difficulty rating, which can be interpreted as follows: "Easy" trails can be completed without difficulty by hikers of all abilities. Hikes rated "moderate" will challenge novices. "Moderately strenuous" hikes will tax even experienced hikers, and "strenuous" trails will push the limits of even the most Herculean traveler.

After this statistical outline section, you'll find directions for **Finding the trailhead,** a narrative hike description, and when significant, a mile-by-mile description of landmarks and trail junctions. We marked trail distances using an instrument called a planimeter, which measures two-dimensional distances on a topographical map. These distances then were corrected for elevation gain or loss and modified where managers had made more precise determinations. The resulting mileages should be looked upon as conservative estimates, however, because they do not always account for small-scale twists and turns or minor ups and downs.

Our interpretive narrative of each hike also includes geologic and ecological features, fishing opportunities, campsites, and other important information. We've added photographs to this guidebook to give readers a visual preview of some of the prominent features seen along the trail.

The maps in this book that depict a detailed close-up of an area use elevation tints, called hypsometry, to portray relief. Each gray tone represents a range of equal elevation, as shown in the scale key with the map. These maps will give you a good idea of elevation gain and loss. The darker tones are lower elevations and the lighter

◀ *An improvised log crossing along Grizzly Bear Creek Trail might help keep your feet dry.*

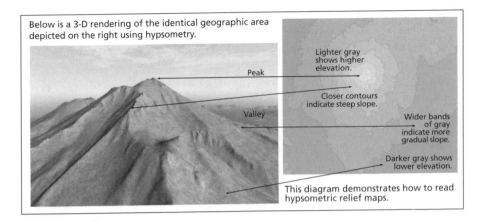

Below is a 3-D rendering of the identical geographic area depicted on the right using hypsometry.

Peak

Valley

Lighter gray shows higher elevation.

Closer contours indicate steep slope.

Wider bands of gray indicate more gradual slope.

Darker gray shows lower elevation.

This diagram demonstrates how to read hypsometric relief maps.

grays are higher elevations. The lighter the tone, the higher the elevation. Narrow bands of different gray tones spaced closely together indicate steep terrain, whereas wider bands indicate areas of more gradual slope. (See the diagram above.)

Maps that show larger geographic areas use shaded, or shadow, relief. Shadow relief does not represent elevation; it demonstrates slope or relative steepness. This gives an almost 3-D perspective of the physiography of a region and will help you see where ranges and valleys are.

This guide is just that: a guide, not the final word on each trail listed here. Use topographic maps and other resources to round out your regional knowledge, and know your own limits and heed them. You'll then enjoy your travels in beautiful Black Hills Country and have a memorable hiking experience.

Clothing and Equipment

Comfortable clothes and footwear do more to make a hike pleasant than nearly any other items of equipment. The great variety of hiking and walking situations make it impossible to cover all personal needs in this introduction, but here are a few suggestions for a hiker's attire: First, dress in layers. The layer closest to your skin should be a light, inner layer made of material that will wick away moisture from the skin. Next should be a warmer, porous layer that can be removed if necessary. Over that wear an outside layer that is wind- and/or rain-proof. This layering system permits you to regulate your temperature easier by putting on or peeling off layers as weather and exertion dictate. Along with these basics, bring along a good rain poncho or coat as part of your standard backpacking equipment. Rain, snow, sleet, and hail are frequent and unpredictable in the Black Hills.

Each hiker seems to have a different idea about what type of footwear she or he should use. Boots or shoes are a matter of personal preference but, regardless of style

A September snowfall tops Crow Peak. ▶

and weight, they should be sturdy and supportive. Many people still wear good leather boots for serious hiking, while others prefer lightweight boots with breathable, water-resistant fabrics. The best advice we can give a beginner is to visit a good outfitter or outdoor-sports store and try on several styles before finally deciding.

We've included a hiker's checklist in appendix A to help you as you pack for your Black Hills trip. We've also listed several good books that discuss equipment in appendix D. Most of these are available in libraries. One of the best is Colin Fletcher's *The Complete Walker III*. Others are available in better sporting-goods stores.

Planning the Hike

Hiking should be fun, even if you hike just for the benefits of physical fitness. To keep it that way, plan hikes that are within your physical ability. Do not attempt long trails or backpacking segments that are more than you can safely accomplish in daylight. Hiking after dark is not only uncomfortable but also dangerous, especially if you are not familiar with the topography and trail conditions. Know the terrain, and study maps before you depart.

Always leave an itinerary with someone before you leave. This should include where you will be hiking, where you will park, your estimated time for completing the trip, and whom to contact if necessary. This will lead help to you if by unlucky chance you have a trail accident, or if there is some other kind of emergency.

Hiking and walking seem so simple they lull hikers into being careless. No hike, whether a day hike or a weeklong backpack trip, should begin without the basic essential of a first-aid kit and simple survival items. Think of it like fastening your seat belt before driving to the corner store—it's just as vital as using it on a 500-mile interstate trip. A first-aid kit is a very personal item, and its contents will depend on each hiker's needs and concerns. However, your kit can be very small and light. For a day hike, it should contain at least adhesive bandages, gauze or gauze compresses, adhesive tape, an Ace or other brand elastic wraparound bandage, aspirin or other pain relievers, antibacterial ointment, moleskin, needles, and scissors (or a pocket knife with scissors). This can all go in a small plastic bag. A first-aid kit for overnight hikes should contain these same things as well as Benadryl or another antihistamine for allergic response, a small packet of meat tenderizer for insect stings, a mild laxative, something to combat diarrhea, and other personal items. A compact snakebite kit that includes an efficient suction device is also a good idea.

Survival kits can and should be simple and efficient. Carry a compact space blanket or large garbage bag, a whistle, waterproof matches or a reliable cigarette lighter, a compass, a high-energy food bar, 10 or 20 feet of light nylon rope, and a small flashlight. These items are essentials. Keep them with you at all times, especially when on side trips away from your backpack or campsite.

And don't forget to bring enough water. The pristine streams and lakes of the Black Hills are quite refreshing but may contain a microorganism called *Giardia lamblia*, which causes severe diarrhea and dehydration in humans. The microorganism is spread through the feces of wild mammals—especially by beavers, which inhabit many of the low-elevation stream systems. Any surface water supply is a potential source of this organism, and hikers who drink from lakes and streams take the risk of contracting the painful symptoms associated with this pestiferous microbe. Water can be rendered safe by boiling it for at least five minutes or by passing it through a filter system with a mesh no larger than 5 micrometers. Iodine tablets and other purification additives are not considered effective against giardia.

A Few More Words of Caution

Weather

Weather in the Black Hills changes frequently and without warning. Winds sweep off the surrounding plains, and temperatures can drop frequently and without warning. While hiking, we encountered snow in early September, and met cold winds accompanied by drenching rains.

Summer is one of the most pleasant times to hike in the Black Hills, but it can also be one of the most awesome. Lightning storms are frequent and can be nerve-racking as we discovered one day while hiking toward the summit of Harney Peak. Streaks of lightning stabbed the suddenly darkened sky. Only later did we learn how to deal with an electrical storm: Seek shelter away from open ground or exposed ridges. Even dropping a few yards off a ridgetop will reduce your risk. In a forest, stay away from single tall trees; look for a cluster of smaller trees instead. Avoid gullies or small basins with water in the bottom, and find a low spot free of standing water. Stay out of shallow caves, crevasses, or overhangs (numerous and inviting in the Black Hills). Ground discharges may leap across the openings. Dry, deep caves offer better protection, but do not touch the walls.

Whether you are in open country or in a shelter during a lightning storm, assume a low crouch with only your feet touching the ground. Put a sleeping pad or pack (make sure it does not have a metal frame or metal components) beneath your feet for added insulation against shock. Do not huddle together; members of a group should stay at least 30 feet apart. Then, if someone is hit, the others can give first aid. In a tent, get in the crouch position in your sleeping bag and keep your feet on a sleeping pad.

Watch for signs of an imminent lightning strike: hair standing on end; an itchy feeling one hiker described as "bugs crawling all over your skin"; an acrid, "hot metal" smell; and buzzing or crackling noises in the air. Tuck into a crouch immediately if any of these signs are present.

If someone in your group is hit by lightning, be prepared to give CPR and first aid for burns and shock. Many victims survive, even from direct hits, especially if help is nearby and CPR is continued. Check the person's breathing and pulse and look for burns or other injuries. There is no danger of electrocution or shock from touching someone who has been struck by lightning.

Hypothermia is another risk in the Black Hills, even in summer, since there are times when the factors contributing to bodily heat loss are present. Cold rains frequently drench the mountains, and it sometimes hails and even snows. Temperatures need not be below freezing for hypothermia to be a threat. Most cases occur when temperatures range between forty and fifty degrees, often coupled with windy and wet conditions—the precise conditions often found during summer in the Black Hills, particularly in August and September.

People who are inappropriately attired and get wet in such inclement weather have set themselves up for hypothermia. Shivering marks the first stage. In advance stages, shivering stops, but only because the body is too weak to keep it up. This stage may be accompanied by slurred speech, clumsiness with the hands, and impaired judgment.

At the first sign of hypothermia, stop and change clothes: Get the victim out of the wet stuff. In more acute conditions, victims should be placed in a sleeping bag with people lying, skin to skin, on either side. Feed conscious victims something warm and sweet, such as hot chocolate—not alcohol. Because acute hypothermia can lead to death, seek medical help.

Wildlife

Nature runs wild in the Black Hills, and hikers may face risks from wildlife or insects. However, unlike other places, bears are not a problem here. No bears remain in the Black Hills, which once provided a prime habitat for them. The last reported sighting of a bear was vague and dates from the late 1980s. Mosquitoes, also a bane in other places, are few. But a few mountain lions make the Black Hills their home. Today lions are protected in South Dakota and can be found in sparsely populated areas, from the pine forests of the Black Hills to the breaks of the Missouri River.

Lion attacks are rare—in truth, you will be fortunate to catch even a brief glimpse of one of these creatures. If you encounter a lion, remain calm. Back away slowly, taking care to make yourself seem as large as possible, yell and shout, but do not run.

A more likely animal encounter in Black Hills Country is with bison. Loose bison often are encountered by hikers in Badlands National Park, Custer State Park, and Wind Cave National Park. Always be aware of the possibility of such encounters. If you do meet up with bison, do not panic. Quietly move away.

Ticks

Close encounters of the more personal kind may come as hikers find themselves carrying ticks. Though the incidence of Lyme disease in the Black Hills is low, ticks are numerous here. Contracting diseases associated with ticks is, therefore, a distinct possibility. Deer ticks can appear any time of year if the temperature is above fifty degrees, even in January and February. If they attach to the skin, they begin to feed.

Custer State Park hosts one of the nation's largest free-roaming herds of bison. Remain alert!

To a tick, blood has the consistency of Jell-O, which it must thin. To do so, ticks inject a saliva that thins the blood and, in doing so, may simultaneously inject a disease-carrying bacteria harbored in its gut. Lyme disease, Rocky Mountain spotted fever, or the newly diagnosed human *granulocytic ehrlichia* infection may result. General symptoms of these diseases include fever with shaking chills and severe muscle pain. Lyme disease also produces a rash on the palms of the hands and soles of the feet, which later spreads to the whole body.

The best way to prevent tick-borne disease is to prevent ticks from latching to the skin. Wear long pants and tuck them into boots or bind bottoms with a rubber band. Wear long-sleeved shirts. Consider using a pesticide containing deet, which you should apply to skin and clothing. At the end of the day, conduct a tick search of your body and clothing.

If you find one, don't panic. The process of transmitting the disease takes hours. To remove a loose tick, flick it off with a fingernail If the tick is firmly imbedded, encourage it to disengage by holding a hot but extinguished matchhead to its back. If the tick does not let go, use tweezers to pinch a small area around the tick's mouth and pull it out. Try not to squeeze the tick's body, since this increases the risk of infection. Finally, clean the wound with an antiseptic.

Snakes

Rattlesnakes are common in the Black Hills, particularly around prairie-dog communities. Though one should always remain alert, given their druthers, rattlesnakes will always retreat at the approach of humans. If you've never heard a rattlesnake rattle, don't worry: You'll recognize it—the sound is unmistakable.

Rattlesnakes strike when angered, and though every few years someone in the Black Hills seems to get bitten, no one has ever died. Nationwide, 15,000 to 20,000 people are bitten each year; only 6 to 10 of these die. Snake venom is relatively slow-acting, allowing victims a chance to acquire medical attention. In 20 percent of snakebite cases, no venom was injected.

Learning to avoid snakes and their bites is relatively simple: Watch where you step or sit down to rest. Wear high leather boots and long pants in snake habitat. Avoid hiking at night. Snakes generally hole up by day, then bask on sun-warmed rocks or sand when temperatures cool in the evening. Snakes generally hunt at night, too, so it is best to sleep in tents with sewn-in floors and zippered doors.

Before proceeding into snake country, bone up on first-aid treatment. Commercial snake-venom extractors are useful if used within the first three minutes. Victims, if alone, should walk slowly to the trailhead and seek immediate medical attention. If accompanying a snakebite victim, anticipate and treat for shock as needed.

Poison Ivy

Poison ivy abounds in the Black Hills, though the male half of this book-writing team, who is particularly susceptible to the ivy's ill effects, has never incurred the rash in the Black Hills despite much off-trail hiking. Hikers easily can learn to identify poison ivy and avoid plants that have shiny foliage of three leaves. Remember the saying, "Leaves of three, let it be."

Vines of poison ivy in the Black Hills sometimes reach shoulder height, particularly along streams such as French Creek in Custer State Park and Beaver Creek in Wind Cave National Park. In fall the plant is particularly deceptive, since its leaves turn a beautiful orange and the plant produces a white berry, somewhat similar to a snowberry.

Though many hikers prefer to wear shorts, to avoid poison ivy, we recommend that you wear long pants. Trails are sometimes narrow and, under those circumstances, skin exposure is almost certain. Use care when selecting "cat holes" to relive yourself. Ivy-induced rashes on the genitals can be particularly troublesome and may require medical attention.

If you suspect you have rubbed against poison ivy, wash the area immediately with water from a canteen or from a nearby stream. Washing within the first ten minutes can often prevent irritation. Ideally, you should place suspect clothing in a

◀ *Poison ivy produces a white berry in the fall that may be*
mistaken for snowberry. Maintain a wary eye.

Mountain bikes are permitted along many Black Hills trails (such as the Grace Coolidge Trail, shown here), except those in national parks and wilderness areas. Bikers are asked to maintain controlled speeds and remain on the lookout for those who may be proceeding at a slower pace.

plastic bag until it can be thoroughly washed either in a stream or (best) by machine. If a rash appears, apply calamine lotion. Persistent rashes may require something stronger, such as a salve containing cortisone. Extreme cases may require a cortisone injection.

Trail Etiquette

Few things are more irritating or distasteful than finding aluminum cans, candy wrappers, and other litter along the trail. "Pack it in, pack it out" should be the working motto of every hiker. This is true for short day hikes as much as for the wilderness backpack trips. Get in the habit of taking an extra garbage bag on hikes just to pick up litter left by unthinking people on the trail. A clean trail is less inviting to those who litter.

Modern, lightweight camp stoves and lanterns eliminate the need for campfires and stone fire rings. Backpack stoves are ideal for wilderness camping or for brewing up a hot cup of coffee or bowl of soup. Open fires are prohibited in most Black Hills areas, further contributing to a philosophy of taking out what you've packed in.

More basic trail etiquette: Much of the Black Hills is a "multiple-use area," meaning that ranchers and their livestock share the fields and woods. Hikers often encounter cattle gates, which should be left—open or closed—as they are found. Multiple use also means that hikers will share the trail with mountain bikers and horse users. Trail etiquette requires that bikers yield to hikers and that bikers and hikers yield to stock and riders. If stock is encountered on the trail, hikers should move quietly to the lower side of the trail to let the stock pass. Horses are sometimes spooked by sudden, unforeseen encounters, so make your presence known.

Trail etiquette also confers the responsibility to care for the environment and respect the rights of others.

Hiking with Children

With the birth of a child, some new parents might think their hiking and backpacking days are over, at least until Junior is old enough to walk several miles and carry a pack. But parents who forgo hiking trips during a child's formative years are missing out on some of the most rewarding and memorable experiences to be enjoyed as a family. The kids also will miss a tremendous learning experience in which they will gain confidence and a growing awareness of the world around them.

Kids can enjoy the backcountry as much as their parents, but they see the world from a different perspective. It's the little things adults barely notice that are so special to children: bugs scampering across the trail, spider webs dripping with morning dew, lizards doing push-ups on a trailside boulder, rocks splashing into a lake, sticks running the rapids of a mountain stream, animal tracks in the sand. These are but a few of the natural wonders kids will enjoy while hiking backcountry trails.

To make the trip fun for the kids, let the young ones set the pace. Until they get older and are able to keep up with their parents, forget about that 30-mile trek to your favorite backcountry campsite. Instead, plan a destination that is only a mile or two from the trailhead. Kids tire quickly and become easily sidetracked, so don't be surprised if you don't make it to your end point. Plan alternative campsites en route to your intended destination.

Help children enjoy the hike and learn about what they see by pointing out special things along the trail. Help them to anticipate what is around the next bend— perhaps a waterfall, or a pond filled with wriggling tadpoles. Make the hike fun and interesting and kids will keep going.

Careful planning that stresses safety will help make your outing an enjoyable one. Young skin is very sensitive to the sun, so always carry a strong sunscreen and apply it to your kids before and during your hike. A good bug repellent, preferably a natural product, should be a standard part of the first-aid kit. Consider bringing a product that helps take the itch and sting out of bug bites. A hat helps keep the sun out of sensitive young eyes, and rain gear is important. Kids seem to have less tolerance to cold than adults, so carry ample clothing.

Needle and spire formations dominate the skyline as you hike in the Cathedral Spires area.

Parents with young children must carry plenty of diapers—and pack them out when they leave. Some children can get wet at night, so extra sleeping clothes are a must. A waterproof pad between the child and the sleeping bag should keep the bag dry. This is vital if you intend to stay out more than one night.

Parents with very young children can find an alternative to baby food in jars to alleviate extra weight. Bring lightweight and inexpensive dry baby foods, to which you just add water.

Allow older children who are able to walk a mile or two to carry their own packs. Some kids will want to bring favorite toys or books along. By carrying these special things themselves, they learn at an early age the advantages of packing light.

Kids may become bored more easily once you arrive in camp, so you may need to put in a little extra effort to keep them occupied. Imaginative games and special foods they don't see at home can make the camping trip a new and fun experience for kids and parents alike. Children learn from their parents by example. Hiking and camping trips are excellent opportunities to teach young ones to tread lightly and minimize their imprint upon the environment.

There are many good camping and hiking areas in the Black Hills where children can experience the fun of seeing a beautiful flower, butterfly, babbling brook, or bluebird bringing food to its young. Seeing a deer bounding away in a woodland setting can be very exciting for a child—and a parent. Many units within the Black Hills have excellent nature trails ideal for beginning hikes. Interpretive programs are conducted by well-trained park naturalists and program specialists. Some units also have backpacking, camping, and hiking programs that teach techniques. These hands-on programs teach beginners how to camp and hike, and how to do it with minimum impact on natural areas. Many of the hikes that follow are suitable for family day hikes or backpacks.

To recap, important considerations to keep in mind when hiking with children are careful planning, stressing safety, and making the trip fun and interesting. There may be extra hassles involved with family hiking trips, but the dividends are immeasurable. Parents will gain a rejuvenated perspective of nature as seen through the eyes of a child. This will reward them each time they venture out on the trail.

Final Notes

Some general information for hikers in the Black Hills: South Dakota fishing licenses are required for all lakes and streams. You can purchase a one-day, five-day, or seasonal license.

Custer State Park holds an annual Buffalo Round-up, usually the last weekend of September. This event is open to the public and is an exciting time for all. The buffalo corrals are located along the Wildlife Loop Road and visitors can watch the bison being driven to the corrals. From elevated platforms, visitors can then see how the bison are culled and inoculated. The Custer State Park annual Arts Festival is held on the same weekend as the Buffalo Round-up. Local artists and artisans are featured, as are bands and singing. A great chili cook-off ends the affair.

Mount Rushmore is the most famous attraction of the Black Hills area, but be sure to include a visit to the memorial (still being carved) to Crazy Horse, located between Hill City and Custer. We suggest that hikers drive as many of the scenic roads of the Black Hills as possible. This will give you a better feel for the whole area and help you pinpoint trails that interest you.

And one last note from the authors: Covering every trail in the Black Hills was not our goal. Many trails cross private lands, and we did not hike any of those. We chose to write up only those trails that are on public land and include only those that we felt gave the best views of each area. We apologize if we've left out your favorite trail or hike. At the same time, we welcome any suggestions or corrections readers might have to offer. Please feel free to write us c/o The Globe Pequot Press/Falcon Guide® or e-mail editorial@GlobePequot.com to share your thoughts.

Map Legend

Boundary

State/National Park

Monument/Preserve

Private

State

Transportation

Interstate ⬣ I 75

Paved 🔷 41

Gravel 29 — 94

Unimproved = = = = = = = =

Selected Hikes

Shared Trail

Other Hikes - - - - - - - - - - - -

Hydrology

Rivers/Creeks

Lake

Waterfall

Physical

Cliff

Mount/Peak ▲

Grids

UTM Coordinates 723000m

Symbols

Accommodation 🛖

Campground ⛺

Tunnel

Dam ▬

Visitor Information ❓

Overlook 👁

Pass)(

Devils Tower ◉

Mount Rushmore 🗻

Parking 🅿

Picnic ⛱

Start of Hike START 🚶

Trail Number ⑤

Turnaround ↻

Structure / Pt. of Interest ■

Amphitheater ▣

Towns / Cities ○

Park Office ◣

Physiography

Terrain (Shaded Relief)

Mountain, Peak, or Butte ▲

Valley

Bearlodge Mountains

The Bearlodge Mountains in the extreme northeast portion of Wyoming make up the northwest section of the Black Hills. The range is just beginning to establish its reputation as home to premier hiking trails. Trails in the area now total 56 miles, including many recently developed routes—some created as recently as 1996. How fortunate we are to have these trails, new and old, which wander through significant segments of natural and historical time! "The Bearlodge Mountains are unique," says Jerry Hagen, coordinator for the Bearlodge trails, "since they are a mosaic of eastern hardwoods and western coniferous forest." Hikers here will pass astonishing vistas.

The Bearlodge range has hosted some intriguing historic events. For long periods the area was home to Native Americans, as evidenced by the thousands of artifacts left over as many years at Vore Buffalo Jump, 12 miles east of Sundance, Wyoming. Archaeologists believe native peoples drove more than 20,000 animals over the jump. Not surprisingly, the Bearlodge Mountains served as the backdrop for a Native American sun-dance ceremony. The event later provided the name for the nearby town of Sundance, Wyoming, long before the notorious "Sundance Kid" served time in the town's jail.

In 1874 the area surrounding the Bearlodge range hosted the Custer Expedition to the Black Hills. U.S. Army general George Armstrong Custer was searching for fortification sites to protect local settlers when he climbed high on Inyan Kara (6,368 feet), a mountain the Native Americans considered sacred, visible from many Bearlodge trails. One of Custer's men, a Colonel Ludlow, inscribed the name G. A. CUSTER and the date 74, on a rock wall on the peak. Today the remains of this etching can be found by those willing to make the proper inquiries and the rigorous climb.

Wagon ruts from the Custer Expedition are still visible in the fields and valleys of the Bearlodge area, as are other trails of early settlers. Following the Custer Expedition, miners and homesteaders began making their way into the mountains here. In 1881 the Ogden family settled in what is now Ogden Canyon, followed by prospector Emil Reuter. Reuter so loved the area that he remained here until his death some thirty-two years after he arrived. Today his grave can be seen along Ogden Canyon Road.

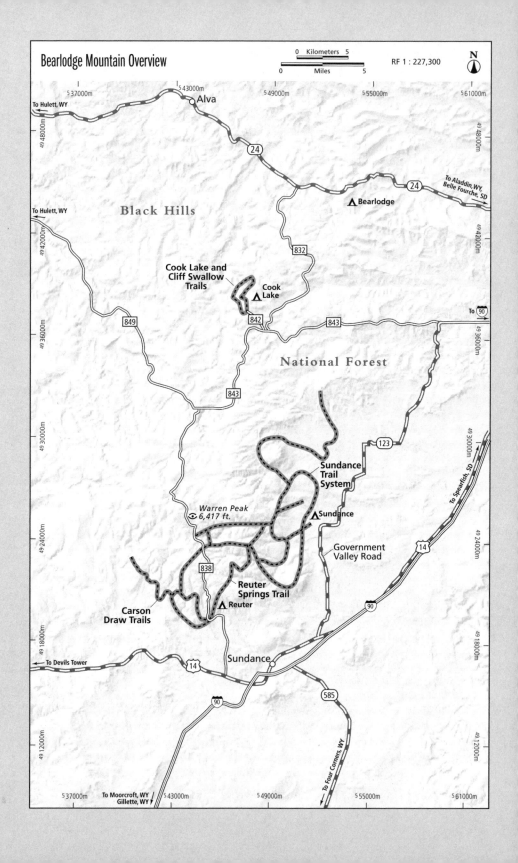

Area ranchers also used the settlers' trails, driving their cattle to water holes deep in the hills. They were followed later by firefighters, who created paths of their own and reinforced already-existing trails. Out of these paths, Forest Service district managers created a trail network, which they categorized into three systems: The **Sundance System** comprises 50.3 miles of trails; the **Carson Draw System** includes 6 trail miles; and the **Cook Lake/Cliff Swallow System** covers 4.5 miles. For greater access, each of the systems has been located near a Forest Service campground.

The Forest Service advises trail users to carry their own water or be prepared to purify water from springs and streams, and to be aware that they may meet up with poison ivy and rattlesnakes. Depending on the trails they take, hikers in the Bearlodge Mountains are rewarded with experiences that range from true adventure to quiet, meditative walks.

Before embarking on one of the many trails within the system, hikers would do well to make the drive to the top of 6,656-foot Warren Peak, 4 miles north of Reuter Campground on Forest Road 838, which is 2.9 miles west of Sundance. From this vantage point, hikers can familiarize themselves with the area's major features, including Devils Tower, the Missouri Buttes, and other significant landmarks. As you hike the rugged Bearlodge Mountains, you'll see these features again and again, and by them you'll soon know the lay of the land.

Sundance is 107 miles west of Rapid City, South Dakota, on Interstate 90 (I–90), 32 miles west of Spearfish, South Dakota, on I–90. From the east, Sundance is 28 miles southeast of Devils Tower, Wyoming, by means of Wyoming Highway 24 (for 6 miles) and U.S. Highway 14 (for 22 miles).

1 Cook Lake and Cliff Swallow Trails

A level lakeshore hike and a longer, moderately difficult path for those interested in natural history.

Start: At Cook Lake, 20 miles north of Sundance.
Distance: 1-mile loop around Cook Lake; 3.5-mile loop on the Cliff Swallow trail; a total distance of 4.5 miles.
Approximate hiking time: ¾ hour for Cook Lake, 1½ to 3 hours for Cliff Swallow hike.
Difficulty: Varies from easy to moderate.
Seasons: Best from late spring into fall.

Other trail users: Horses.
Land status: Black Hills National Forest.
Fees and permits: N/A
Maps: Free trail brochure from the Forest Service office in Sundance; Black Hills National Forest map.
Trail contact: Bearlodge Ranger District, U.S. Highway 14 East, Box 680, Sundance, WY 82729; (307) 283-1361.

Finding the trailheads: Both trails are accessed from Cook Lake, 20 miles north of Sundance. Find the Forest Service office on US 14 (Cleveland Street) near the east end of Sundance. From the office, proceed 2.9 miles west on US 14 to Forest Road 838 north. Follow FR 838 for 2.6 miles to Reuter Campground, which serves as a nice base.

From the campground, go north on FR 838 to Forest Road 843. Take FR 843 north to Forest Road 842, and follow this road into the Cook Lake area and campground. Access the Cook Lake Trail at any point around the lake. Trailheads for the Cliff Swallow Trail are located on the north side of the lake and depart from both the campground and the road. These spur trails quickly merge with the trail proper.

The Hike

The Cook Lake Trail is self-explanatory, following a level route around the shore of Cook Lake. The lake is stocked with brown and rainbow trout; anglers will need a Wyoming fishing license.

The Cliff Swallow Trail is intended for recreational hikers with an interest in natural history. If hikers take the loop hike going counterclockwise, the trail begins by paralleling Beaver Creek. Bur oak, aspen, and birch line the trail, while bluffs filled with cliff-swallow nesting holes rise on the east side of the stream. Above the bluffs, turkey vultures ride the thermals. In fall, shrubs at trailside adorn the route with clusters of red berries. The area serves as prime deer habitat.

The trail is well marked with brown signs depicting cliff swallows. Along the way beaver dams impound the nearby stream, adding considerable interest to the outing. Hikers should search the stream for water ouzels, also known as "dippers" because

This fawn was spied in the grasslands of Bearlodge Mountains.

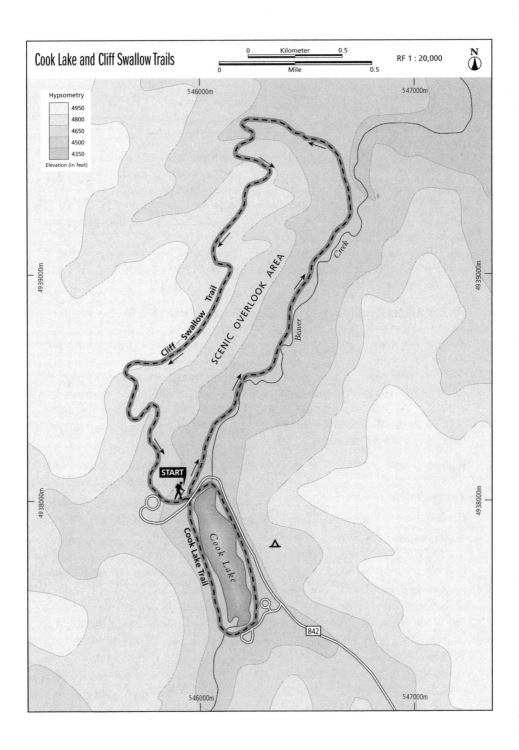

Cook Lake and Cliff Swallow Trails

Kilometer
0   0.5
Mile
0   0.5

RF 1 : 20,000

N

Hypsometry

	4950
	4800
	4650
	4500
	4350

Elevation (in feet)

546000m

547000m

4939000m

4939000m

4938000m

4938000m

546000m

547000m

Cliff Swallow Trail

SCENIC OVERLOOK AREA

Beaver Creek

START

Cook Lake Trail

Cook Lake

842

of their tendency to perch on a rock and dip up and down into the water as they peer into the depths for insects.

Two miles from the trailhead, the path begins to wind uphill and away from the creek. The trail ascends a series of switchbacks, none of which is particularly strenuous. The trail crests about 0.5 mile from the creek, providing excellent views of the cliffs that serve as a seasonal residence for cliff swallows.

Miles and Directions

0.0 Start at the Cliff Swallow trailhead.

2.5 The trail crests.

3.5 The loop is completed back at the trailhead.

2 Carson Draw Trails

Woods and canyon trails designed for four-season use, offering solitude in the Wyoming Black Hills.

Start: At Reuter Campground, 5.5 miles from Sundance, Wyoming.
Distance: 4-mile lollipop.
Approximate hiking time: 2 to 4 hours.
Difficulty: Easy to moderate.
Highest elevation: 5,700 feet.
Seasons: All year.
Other trail users: Horses, bikers, cross-country skiers.

Land status: National forest.
Fees and permits: N/A
Maps: Free trail map available at the Sundance Forest Service office; Black Hills National Forest map.
Trail contact: Bearlodge Ranger District, U.S. Highway 14 East, Box 680, Sundance, WY 82729; (307) 283-1361.

Finding the trailhead: From the Forest Service office on US 14 (Cleveland Street) near the east end of Sundance, proceed 2.9 miles west on US 14 to Forest Road 838 north. Follow the road 2.6 miles to Reuter Campground, where the trail system begins.

The Hike

The Carson Draw Trails primarily have been used by cross-country skiers in the past, but these trails offer backwoods treks of great beauty and solitude year-round. Hikers and bikers can make a loop hike within the 6-mile trail system or go on a series of one-way hikes. You may also link up to the Sundance Trail System. Be alert for the presence of horse riders, who also use these nonmotorized trails.

The system's main trail departs from the campground and heads southwest before swinging northwest. The path winds through prime habitat for elk, deer, and songbirds in stands of ponderosa pine, oak, and aspen. After about 1 mile hikers will

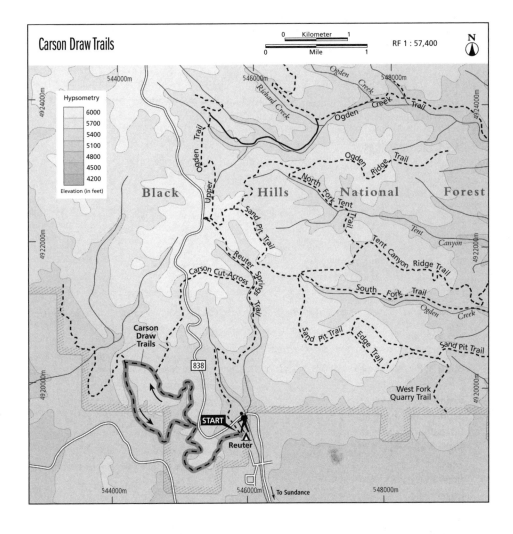

encounter a loop trail, which lies in the center of the 6 miles of trail here. By hiking north (counterclockwise) on the loop, you can circle around and return to your starting point. Another option is to branch off the loop after almost 1 mile and head north to the Carson Cut-Across, which connects with Reuter Springs Trail. Hikers with a good sense of direction (or a compass) can create their own circuits here.

Miles and Directions

0.0 Start at the trailhead at Reuter Campground.

1.0 Join the loop by turning right.

1.8 The Carson Draw to Carson Cut-Across is an option.

4.0 Return to the trailhead after following the loop.

3 Sundance Trail System

A series of loops among the newest trails in the Bearlodge Mountains, extending a total of 50.3 miles.

Start: Suggested start is at Sundance Campground and trailhead.
Distance: Loop A, 14.4 miles; Loop B, 9.2 miles.
Approximate hiking time: 6 to 7 hours for each loop.
Difficulty: Easy to moderately strenuous.
Highest elevation: 6,400 feet.
Seasons: Spring through fall.

Other trail users: Horses.
Land status: National forest.
Fees and permits: N/A
Maps: Free trail map from the Sundance Forest Service office; Black Hills National Forest map.
Trail contact: Bearlodge Ranger District, U.S. Highway 14 East, Box 680, Sundance, WY 82729; (307) 283-1361.

Finding the trailheads: Suggested access is from Sundance Campground and trailhead. From the Forest Service office in Sundance, go 0.3 mile east to Government Valley Road. Follow this road 2.1 miles north to the campground. Hikers could also use the Reuter Springs Trailhead across from Reuter Campground to access the trail system.

The Hike

Loop A departs from Sundance Campground and proceeds westerly along the Sundance Trail until it connects 1.2 miles later with the Tent Canyon Trail. Follow Tent Canyon for 4.1 miles until intersecting with the Ogden Creek Trail. Take this trail west for 3.6 miles until linking with the Upper Ogden Trail. Proceed south on Upper Ogden Trail for 1.3 miles to where the trail meets the Sand Pit Trail, at which point hikers should head east. About 1 mile later hikers will connect with the Tent Canyon Ridge Trail and should follow this 2 miles to the Sundance Trail, which returns you to the campground.

A shorter route, **Loop B** also begins on the Sundance Trail and follows it for 1.2 miles. To make this loop, hikers then proceed north on the Tent Canyon Trail for 1 mile to a junction with the Tent Canyon Ridge Trail, from the west. Follow the latter for 3.3 miles to the intersection with the Sand Pit Trail. Proceed south, then southeast, on the Sand Pit Trail. After 2.5 miles you'll reach the Sundance Trail, which you can take back to the campground for a total loop hike of 9.2 miles.

Miles and Directions

Loop A

0.0 Start at the Sundance trailhead at Sundance Campground.
1.2 Follow the Tent Canyon Trail north.

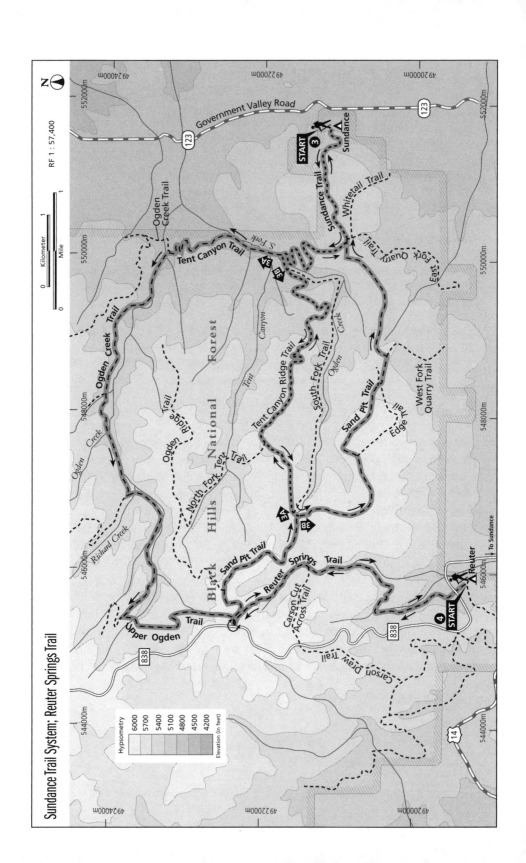

Sundance Trail System; Reuter Springs Trail

RF 1 : 57,400

3.0 At the junction stay to the left on Ogden Creek Trail.

6.3 Link with Upper Ogden Trail and proceed south.

7.6 Link with Sand Pit Trail and proceed southeast.

8.9 At the junction take a left onto Tent Canyon Ridge Trail.

12.2 Rejoin Tent Canyon, turning right to walk south.

13.2 Retrace your steps eastward on Sundance Trail.

14.4 Arrive back at Sundance trailhead.

Loop B

0.0 Start at the Sundance trailhead.

1.2 Proceed north on the Tent Canyon Trail.

2.2 Follow the Tent Canyon Ridge Trail west.

5.5 Follow the Sand Pit Trail south, then southeast.

8.0 Reconnect with the Sundance Trail.

9.2 Arrive back at Sundance trailhead.

4 Reuter Springs Trail

A hike through a pine forest on a ridge above Reuter Canyon.

See map on page 26
Start: At Reuter Campground.
Distance: 5.8 miles out and back.
Approximate hiking time: 3 to 4 hours.
Difficulty: Moderately easy.
Seasons: Late spring through fall.
Other trail users: Horses, mountain bikers.

Land status: National forest.
Fees and permits: N/A
Maps: USDA Forest Service brochure from Sundance Forest Service office.
Trail contact: Bearlodge Ranger District, U.S. Highway 14 East, Box 680, Sundance, WY 82729; (307) 283-1361.

Finding the trailhead: From the Forest Service office on US 14 (Cleveland Street) near the east end of Sundance, proceed 2.9 miles west on US 14 to Forest Road 838 north. Follow the road 2.6 miles to Reuter Campground. The trail is accessed from FR 838, across the road from the campground entrance.

The Hike

The Reuter Springs Trail is suitable for hikers, horseback riders, and mountain bikers. Portions of this fairly new trail were developed in 1995.

The trail proceeds north from the trailhead and follows the ridge above Reuter Canyon. After 0.75 mile, openings in the ponderosa woods grant beautiful southern vistas of surrounding mountains and ranchlands. Signs of deer and elk are plentiful. The trail continues, winding around the canyon with moderate ascents.

At the northern terminus, hikers have several options. You can link up with one of several of the Sundance trails, which head north and east, or return to Reuter Campground. From there you can cross FR 838, walk south on the road for 0.5 mile, and take the Carson Draw ski trail back to the campground again, paralleling the road. Another option is to simply retrace your route.

Miles and Directions

0.0 Start at Reuter Campground Trailhead, 5.5 miles from Sundance, Wyoming.

0.75 Enjoy the southern view.

2.0 Carson Cut-Across comes in from the left; stay right.

2.9 Reach the end of Reuter Springs Trail.

5.8 Return to the trailhead.

Bear Butte State Park

We did not think of the great open plains, the beautiful rolling hills, and the winding streams with tangled growth, as wild. Earth was bountiful and we were surrounded with the blessings of the great Mystery.

—Luther Standing Bear
Lakota Nation

Bear Butte is not a butte at all, but a mountain of igneous rock, formed in much the same way many other area mountains were sculpted. Bear Butte was born more than two million years ago when molten lava pushed into the surrounding land. Over the eons, the softer sedimentary rock engulfing the lava washed away, exposing the igneous core and creating a formation known as a laccolith. Bear Butte shares this manner of development with Crow Peak, among other local landmarks.

Although Bear Butte is not part of the Black Hills proper, its inclusion in this guidebook is justified for several reasons. Historically, it stood as a landmark, pointing the way for many early day "hikers" trudging across the prairie in search of gold, furs, or homesteads in the Black Hills. Because of its prominence and beauty, the butte has served as a beacon. It still does. Rising 1,200 feet above the plains, it is located just outside the northeast corner of the Black Hills, approximately 6 miles northeast of Sturgis, South Dakota, and is part of Bear Butte State Park. Bear Butte is also the northern terminus for the Centennial Trail, which courses through the Black Hills.

In 1965 the mountain was designated a registered National Landmark because of its exceptional value in illustrating a unique segment of the natural history of the United States. In 1973 Bear Butte was placed on the National Register of Historic Places because of its service as a beacon and its spiritual significance to Native Americans. The mountain was a magnet for Native Americans. The Cheyenne called the mountain Noavosse, meaning "Good Mountain," while the Lakota called it Mato Paha, or "Bear Mountain."

Native Americans who came here long ago generally climbed the mountain for spiritual reasons. Today they do much the same. We who follow in their footsteps

To Native Americans, Bear Butte remains a spiritual area, one in which trails approach sweat lodges and other prayer areas. Respect cautionary signs that ask for silence and for unauthorized hikers to maintain their distance.

should do so with a degree of humility, for Bear Butte is to many a cathedral, designated as such with much the same sense of reverence that leaders from, for example, the Christian community have declared certain temples to be sacred. We discuss the trail here, overcoming our concerns that publicity will contribute to a desecration of this Native American shrine. We believe and hope that as we hikers observe a sense of decorum, our presence will become acceptable.

Spiritual leaders ask that as you hike the trail at Bear Butte, you comport yourself with reserve and some degree of somberness. Doing so, you may also feel the spirituality of the mountain. Observe OFF-LIMITS signs and do not intrude on those who may be praying and meditating. Take only scenic photos and none of ceremonial objects or the Native Americans themselves.

Native Americans have tied prayer flags and bundles in trees over the many years of use, and these now number in the thousands. If viewed in the spirit of a naturalist—as one communing with nature—the flags' presence adds to the beauty of the hike and to an appreciation of its antiquity. Please do not disturb them.

5 Bear Butte

A beautiful, invigorating hike from the base to the peak of a sacred mountain. The trail winds through a pine forest; many tree branches are draped with prayer flags and ceremonial objects.

Start: At the trailhead at Bear Butte State Park, located 8 miles from Sturgis, South Dakota.
Distance: 3.4 miles out and back.
Approximate hiking time: 2 to 3 hours.
Difficulty: Moderately strenuous to strenuous, due to the sharp ascent over a relatively short distance.
Highest elevation: 4,426 feet.
Seasons: Best from late spring through fall.
Other trail users: Hikers only.

Land status: Bear Butte State Park.
Fees and permits: N/A
Maps: USDAFS Centennial Trail User Guide. Bear Butte State Park management has provided a sketch map of the trails on an information sign at the trailhead. A map of the hike may also be obtained at the Bear Butte Education Center, where the hike begins.
Trail contact: Bear Butte State Park, P.O. Box 688, Sturgis, SD 57785; (605) 347-5240.

Finding the trailhead: From Sturgis (17 miles east of Spearfish on Interstate 90, or 27 miles west of Rapid City), take South Dakota Highway 34 east for 4 miles to South Dakota Highway 79. Go north on SD 79 for 4 miles to the sign on the right for Bear Butte State Park, where there is camping along the shores of Bear Butte Lake (across SD 79 from the park entrance). The trailhead is located at the Bear Butte Education Center, a 1-mile drive up the road from where you turn off SD 79.

Another trailhead is located directly across SD 79 from the turn-in for the state park. This is the Centennial Trail, and hikers could add 1.5 miles to their hike by departing from here.

The Hike

The Bear Butte Education Center explains more about the area's natural history and its significance to Native Americans. Outside the education center is a bust of Frank Fools Crow (1809–1889), the ceremonial chief of the Teton Lakota Sioux and a nephew of Black Elk. The park's relatively short, steep trail provides an excursion imbued with beauty and spirituality. Simultaneously the trail provides access to the top of Bear Butte, which offers unspoiled panoramic views.

In 1996 a massive fire ravaged much of Bear Butte, consuming about 90 percent of the ponderosa-pine trees on the mountain. One trail, the Ceremonial Trail, is now permanently closed to hikers. The effects of the fire will remain for many, many years, but the surrounding grasslands are rebounding quickly. The natural process of fire and its part in ecology is evidenced in a huge way, one that you will see as you hike.

Begin the hike on the Summit Trail, which is well marked at the trailhead at the education center and serves a dual purpose here with the Centennial Trail. This trail lies to the west of the closed Ceremonial Trail. The dirt path is wide and ascends

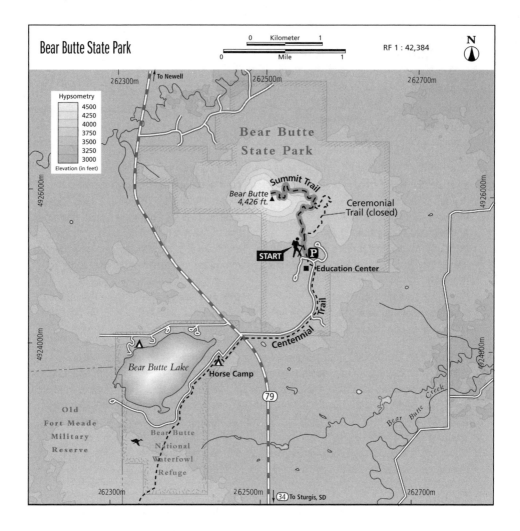

through stands of pine, crossing talus slopes and offering numerous switchbacks. As you begin the trek, look east toward the closed Ceremonial Trail. The hill on the right (east) is called Teaching Hill. This is where the Sioux leader Crazy Horse spoke to tribes gathered for a huge council in 1857. The meeting unified the Sioux in their resolve not to sell the Black Hills to the U.S. government. Here, jagged limestone formations rise in front of the trail.

Follow the Summit Trail for 1 mile north to the point where the trail swings left (west). At this point hikers can continue up to the peak on the Summit Trail (which is also the Centennial Trail) or descend back to the parking lot, making a shorter hike of 2 miles. However, it is well worth the effort to continue to the peak.

The Summit Trail continues winding through pines and around the cliffs, with numerous switchbacks. Where washouts might occur, park managers have placed log

Bust of Frank Fools Crow is located at the education center at Bear Butte State Park.

steps. The lookout platform is reached after 1.3 miles and hikers find themselves standing above an enormous talus slope. Hikers reach the summit 0.4 mile later and are rewarded with commanding 360-degree views of bison, ponds, farms, and cattle; of the Black Hills looming to the southwest; and of the Badlands to the east.

From the peak, retrace the hike along the Summit Trail and descend back to the trailhead.

Miles and Directions

0.0 Start at the Summit Trail, going north from the education center.

1.0 Continue left (west) on the Summit Trail.

1.3 Arrive at the overlook, standing above the talus slope.

1.7 You've reached the summit of Bear Butte.

3.4 Return to the trailhead.

NOTE: Bear Butte Lake lies nearby to the south. There you will find a quiet, pretty 2.5-mile trail encircling the lake (this also connects with the Centennial Trail). A small campground sits on the lakeshore, with fifteen sites. Peaceful fishing is found in the lake and there is also a wheelchair-accessible fishing pier. There is a horse camp on the southeast side of the lake, but the portion of the park east of SD 79 is closed to horses.

SAGE ADVICE On the day of our hike, a mist shrouded the land but did not obscure the distant features. Rather, it combined with the golden leaves and served to heighten the mystery and spirituality of the area. I met Ralph Red Fox at Bear Butte on another day, in September, when snow was falling. He must have noticed the dreamcatcher hanging on the mirror in my van, since he waved at me as I stepped from the vehicle. His brown face was lined, and his head was crowded with a full crop of black hair tinged with silver. He said he was traveling home to Idaho but had stopped at Bear Butte for spiritual rejuvenation. We spoke quietly for a few moments, and then he said he would be returning in the evening to participate in a sweat lodge ceremony and that I was welcome to join him.

I thanked Red Fox but told him I could not make a commitment. "The weather," I said, motioning to the falling snow, covering the leaves of green and gold.

He asked me to walk with him for a moment down a trail, where he picked some sage. He rolled the fragrant leaves between his palms. Then he moved his hands in the four directions and asked me to meditate with him. Finally, Red Fox placed the sage in my left palm and crossed my right palm over the left, joining my hands. "Burn this for good luck as you travel," he said.

I thanked him but said little. I wished I had something to give him in return.

Devils Tower National Monument

Devils Tower is 27 miles northwest of Sundance, Wyoming, along U.S. Highway 14 and Wyoming Highway 24. It is 107 miles west and north of Rapid City, South Dakota. Take Interstate 90 (I–90) west from Rapid City for 80 miles to US 14; go north on US 14 for 21 miles to WY 24. Go north on WY 24 for 6 miles to the entrance gate.

Devils Tower rises abruptly 867 feet from its base in northeast Wyoming, looming 1,267 feet above the Belle Fourche River. The national monument—our nation's first—looms high above the land, and in so doing makes us wonder endlessly about its origin. Hikers who tread these trails walk through millions of years of the earth's past as well as more recent human history. Because of its imposing nature and stable rock, 4,000 to 5,000 climbers attempt to scale its heights each year. The tower was first climbed on July 4, 1893, with the aid of a ladder. Climbing is allowed twelve months a year, with a voluntary closure during the month of June out of respect for Native American religious practices. Each spring the west face of the tower is closed to protect nesting falcons.

Because of the tower's shape and numerous striations, Native Americans sought spiritual interpretations of this most prominent of Wyoming edifices. In his book *The Way to Rainy Mountain,* N. Scott Momaday, a Pulitzer prize–winning novelist, recalled a story told by his grandmother. Her words carried a legend of a boy who had been turned into a bear:

> Eight children were there at play, seven sisters and their brother. Suddenly the boy was struck dumb; he trembled and began to run upon his hands and feet. His fingers became claws, and his body was covered with fur. . . . The sisters were terrified; they ran, and the bear after them. They came to the stump of

All trails provide views of Devils Tower, some close up.

a great tree, and the tree spoke to them. It bade them climb upon it, and as they did so it began to rise into the air. The bear came to kill them, but they were just beyond its reach. It reared against the tree and scored the bark all around with its claws. The seven sisters were borne into the sky, and they became the stars of the Big Dipper.

Because of this legend, so eloquently presented by Momaday, Native Americans once referred to Devils Tower as Mateo Teepee, or "Bear's Lodge."

As appealing as the legend is, geologic science offers a somewhat different version of the tower's origin. Geologists say that forces deep within the earth pushed molten rock up until it was embraced by surrounding landforms. As the molten mass cooled, it condensed and cracked along joints, creating four-, five-, and six-sided rock columns—the striations you can see on the tower today. (These columns do occasionally fall, as evidenced by the piles of rocks that rim the tower's base. However, tests conducted to age lichens growing on the fallen rocks suggest the last column to fall did so about ten thousand years ago.)

Devils Tower National Monument Overview

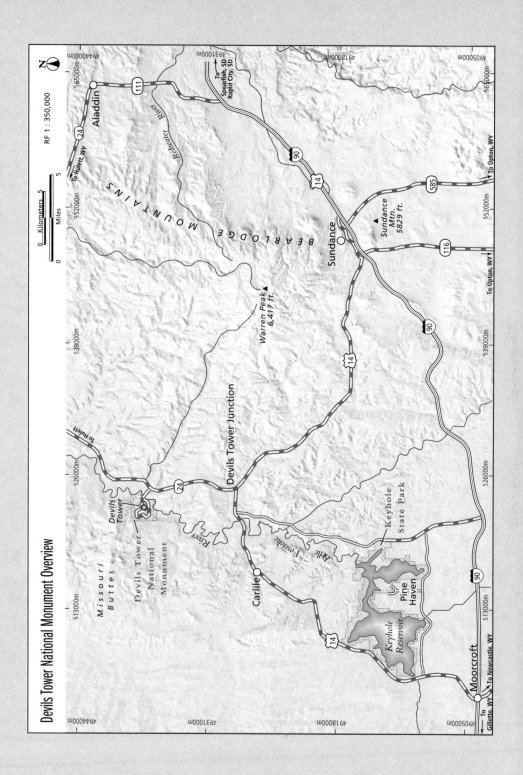

RF 1 : 350,000

Next came the forces of erosion. Since the molten intrusion was harder than the rock and soil of the surrounding landscape, water and wind acted on the softer soil and wore it away. With time—about sixty million years—soil and rocks that had once engulfed the molten columns melted away, leaving only the massive, weather-resistant projection that we see now. In human terms, the immense time frame for such sculpting of Devils Tower suggests inexorable forces. These processes are still in action, though the Black Hills are in no danger of losing the massive tower that dominates Wyoming's northeastern landscape anytime soon.

The monolith has long been revered by Native Americans, and in recent years some shift in management has occurred. Today the monument is managed for its spiritual significance as well as its status as a national monument. Signs near the tower remind visitors not to disturb prayer flags and bundles.

Although many come here to scale Devils Tower, the landscape surrounding the tower should not go unnoticed. Almost 8 miles of trails exist in the national monument. With the exception of one trail, all circle Devils Tower, providing views from every point of the compass. The trails here also provide exquisite, sweeping views of the nearby Belle Fourche River.

Simultaneously, they provide an opportunity for detailed studies of black-tailed prairie dogs and other Great Plains residents. Along the monument's trail, prairie dogs are easily approached; listen to their various calls as you hike the trail. More than seven distinctive chirps have been identified. If a coyote approaches or a hawk is spotted circling overhead, out goes an alarm signal, distinguished by two high-pitched notes. Likewise prairie dogs emit calls signifying contentment. While hiking in the prairie-dog colonies, be aware that prairie rattlesnakes and black widow spiders make their homes in abandoned holes and tunnels. You may find nature's various nuances to be just as interesting as watching the many tower climbers.

The National Park Service lists five trails at the monument, totaling nearly 8 miles. All are well marked and maintained. All trails at Devils Tower are relatively short, and though several climb rather steeply, none do so for long. As a result, hikers need not possess Herculean strength or endurance. Anyone in reasonably good shape can hike here, even though trails such as the Red Beds Trail make quick elevation gains, climbing in places as much as 400 feet in short distances. As a result, we believe certain Devils Tower trails should be ranked moderately strenuous.

6 Tower Trail

A popular circuit trail around the base of Devils Tower.

Start: At the visitor center, which is 3 miles west of the entrance station.
Distance: 1.25-mile loop.
Approximate hiking time: 1 hour.
Difficulty: Easy.
Seasons: Late spring through fall.
Other trail users: Hikers only.
Land status: National monument.

Fees and permits: Climbing fees and permits.
Traffic: Heavy.
Maps: Free trail brochure with map available at entrance gate and visitor center.
Trail contact: Devils Tower National Monument, P.O. Box 8, Devils Tower, WY 82714; (307) 467-5283.

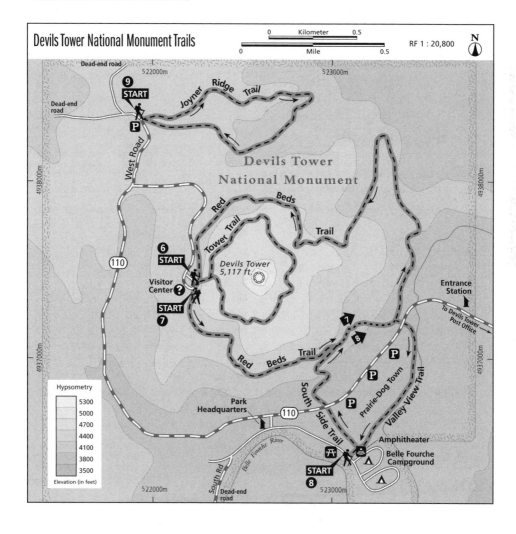

Finding the trailhead: The trail begins at the visitor center, which is 3 miles from the entrance gate.

The Hike

The Tower Trail is perhaps the area's most popular because it most closely rings the base of Devils Tower and provides hikers with an almost bird's-eye view of climbers as they scale the vertical columns. It makes no difference which direction you go. Along the way the park provides benches and interpretive signs. About midway the park provides a mounted set of viewing binoculars.

The path wanders through boulder fields and passes through stands of ponderosa pine, typical of other Black Hills vegetation. The trail also approaches columns that have sloughed off over the millennia and which, in turn, have been modified by the weather. Geologically, this trail excites those with a scientific bent and stirs the imagination in all who hike here.

The entire trail is paved, though somewhat bumpy. On the southeast side a viewing tube focuses on the remains of the old ladder used in 1893 for the first tower climb. Rock doves wing along the columns, and vultures often mass near the top.

7 Red Beds Trail

A longer hike around the tower base than the Tower Trail, past red sandstone formations and a prairie-dog town.

See map on page 39
Start: From the trailhead at the visitor center or from one of the park's other trails that depart from the campground located about 0.5 mile from the entrance station.
Distance: 2.8-mile loop.
Approximate hiking time: 2 to 2½ hours.
Difficulty: Easy to moderately strenuous.
Seasons: Best from late spring through fall.

Other trail users: Hikers only.
Land status: National monument.
Fees and permits: N/A
Traffic: Moderate.
Maps: Free trail brochure with map available at entrance gate and visitor center.
Trail contact: Devils Tower National Monument, P.O. Box 8, Devils Tower, WY 82714; (307) 467-5283.

Finding the trailhead: The trail can be accessed from the visitor center, which is 3 miles west of the entrance gate, or from one of the park's other trails that depart from the campground located about 0.5 mile from the entrance station.

The Hike

The Red Beds Trail also rings Devils Tower, but from a greater distance. Beginning at the visitor center and proceeding south (counterclockwise), the trail descends slightly. Rock formations soon obscure Devils Tower. In 0.7 mile the trail skirts a prairie-dog community then lives up to its name as it passes through formations of red rocks (the red beds).

In another 0.5 mile the trail parallels the Belle Fourche River, then ascends several hundred feet where it once again approaches Devils Tower.

Miles and Directions

0.0   Start at the visitor center.

0.7   The trail skirts a prairie-dog town.

1.2   The trail parallels the Belle Fourche River.

2.8   Reapproach Devils Tower.

8 South Side and Valley View Trails

Two short, scenic trails near the tower's base, which combine to make a loop.

See map on page 39
Start: From the Devils Tower amphitheater.
Distance: 1.2-mile loop.
Approximate hiking time: 1 to 1½ hours.
Difficulty: Easy.
Seasons: Best from late spring through fall.
Other trail users: Hikers only.

Land status: National monument.
Fees and permits: N/A
Maps: Free trail brochure with map available at entrance gate and visitor center.
Trail contact: Devils Tower National Monument, P.O. Box 8, Devils Tower, WY 82714; (307) 467-5283.

Finding the trailhead: Both trails begin at the Devils Tower amphitheater, which is near the campground, about 0.5 mile from the monument's entrance.

The Hike

Each of the South Side and Valley View Trails is a 0.6-mile route that can be walked individually as an out-and-back if hikers insist on maintaining the integrity of each trail's name. Both trails wander through a town of black-tailed prairie dogs. The Valley View Trail lives up to its name by providing elevated views of the nearby river and valley.

We suggest hiking both trails as one clockwise loop. Begin your hike at the amphitheater at the north end of the campground. Hiking clockwise, access the South Side Trail to the left (north). You'll pass an active prairie-dog town on your right and, within 0.25 mile, will cross Wyoming Highway 110. The trail now heads northeast. In another 0.25 mile the Red Beds Trail comes in from your left (west). Stay to the right (east) here on the Red Beds Trail for about 0.25 mile. The Red Beds Trail then continues north; here, you take the Valley View Trail to your right (south) and soon cross

WY 110 once again. The trail now parallels the prairie dog town to your right and ends a little more than a 0.25 mile later back at the amphitheater.

Those not insistent on hiking each trail by name might consider departing the Valley View Trail and linking with the Red Beds Trail, which circles Devils Tower and then returns you to the campground by following the South Side Trail for a total hike of 3 miles.

Miles and Directions

0.0 Start at amphitheater at north end of campground.

0.25 Cross WY 110.

0.5 The Red Beds Trail comes in from the left (west). Access this trail to your right (east).

0.75 The Red Beds Trail continues north; at this point, take the Valley View Trail to your right (south).

0.85 Cross WY 110 once again; continue on Valley View Trail for a little more than a 0.25 mile.

1.2 Return to the amphitheater.

9 Joyner Ridge Trail

A loop hike that provides more distant perspectives of Devils Tower and stunning views of the monument's three major ecosystems.

See map on page 39
Start: On West Road, 2.5 miles from the entrance station.
Distance: 1.5-mile loop.
Approximate hiking time: 1 to 2 hours.
Difficulty: Easy to moderately strenuous.
Seasons: Best from spring through fall.
Other trail users: Hikers only.

Land status: National monument.
Fees and permits: N/A
Maps: Free trail brochure with map available at entrance gate and visitor center.
Trail contact: Devils Tower National Monument, P.O. Box 8, Devils Tower, WY 82714; (307) 467-5283.

Finding the trailhead: Access this trail by following the park's road west from the entrance station for 2 miles until it intersects with West Road, on the left. Take West Road 0.5 mile to the trailhead.

The Hike

The loop known as Joyner Ridge Trail is most easily hiked in a clockwise direction. Hikers pass through the three major Devils Tower ecosystems on this route, including prairie, riparian, and ponderosa-pine habitats. Deer abound throughout the area. The trail is well marked with signs along the way, interpreting the natural communities and enhancing nature's abundant manifestations. Stay alert for prairie rattlesnakes.

Spearfish Area

The Spearfish Canyon area is so special that a National Scenic Byway winds 18 miles through the canyon walls and tree-covered slopes, providing a tour of unparalleled beauty. Hikers would be wise to drive this road, since it gives an excellent overview of this section of the Black Hills, which is managed as part of Black Hills National Forest. To access the National Scenic Byway, take U.S. Highway 14A from Interstate 90 (I–90) in Spearfish.

Spearfish Canyon formations began to take shape thirty million to sixty million years ago. Geologically, three types of rocks dominate the canyon's walls and can be clearly viewed in several places. The top (and thickest and oldest) layer is of the Paha Sapa limestone and is usually gray. The middle layer is Englewood limestone and consists of reddish hues. The bottom is brown, layered, and referred to as Deadwood shale. Vertically formed dark gray rocks called igneous intrusions may also be seen in some areas. Bridal Veil Falls drops from a formation that is a prime example of this condition.

Botanically, four distinctly different vegetative regions thrive in the canyon, which in itself is unusual. The area is a meeting place for plants, trees, and bushes from the Great Plains, the Rocky Mountains, and the Eastern deciduous and Northern forests. No clear explanation exists for such diversity, though it probably derives from ancient climatic changes.

Another novelty, according to one brochure, is that Spearfish Creek is the only known river in the region that freezes from the bottom up. Just how the creek actually received its name is not known, but it is said that Native Americans liked to spear the native long-nosed ace and mountain suckers in the unclouded waters. Today the clear waters are filled with rainbow, brown, and brook trout, which were introduced in 1899.

Several trails exist side-by-side in Spearfish Canyon, including the Little Spearfish Trail, the Rimrock Trail Upper Loop, and the Rimrock Trail Lower Loop. These are high-country hikes, passing through stands of aspen, birch, pine, and spruce. Each provides both beauty and tranquillity. The winter scenes of the movie *Dances with Wolves* were filmed in this canyon, and with a little imagination the tepees pitched in the snow and the drama portrayed of those long-ago times can be conjured easily. A small sign indicates the filming area, but there is fortunately no other hype about what occurred here.

Two campgrounds, Rod and Gun Campground and Timon Campground, are free after Labor Day; water is usually turned off at that time. Trail users who are not camping should avoid parking in the campgrounds during the fee season (Memorial Day through Labor Day).

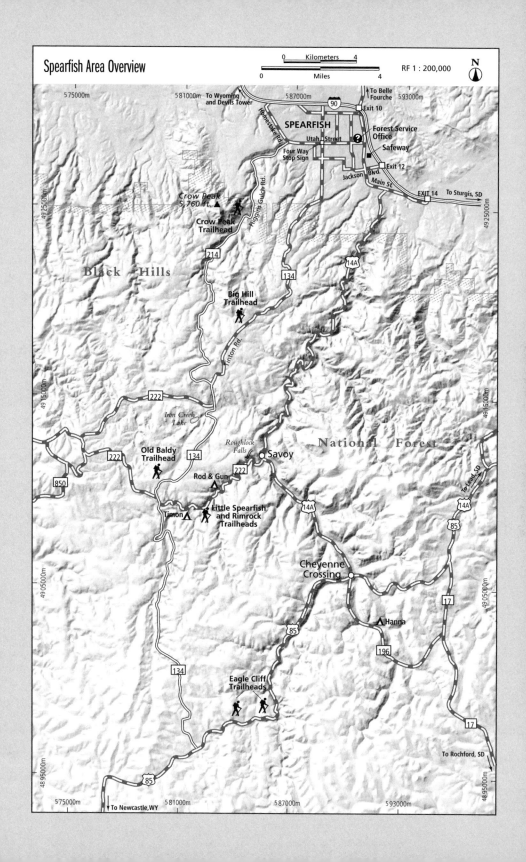

Spearfish Area Overview

Kilometers
0   4
Miles
0   4

RF 1 : 200,000

N

To Wyoming
and Devils Tower

To Belle
Fourche

Exit 10

SPEARFISH

Forest Service
Office

Utah Street

Safeway

Four Way
Stop Sign

Exit 12

Jackson Blvd.

Main St

EXIT 14   To Sturgis, SD

14A

Crow Peak
5,760 ft.

Crow Peak
Trailhead

Higgins Gulch Rd.

Homestake Rd.

Black Hills

214

134

Big Hill
Trailhead

Tinton Rd.

222

Iron Creek
Lake

National Forest

Old Baldy
Trailhead

Roughlock
Falls

Savoy

To Lead, SD

222

134

850

Rod & Gun

222

14A

Little Spearfish
and Rimrock
Trailheads

14A

85

Timon

Cheyenne
Crossing

17

85

134

Hanna

196

Eagle Cliff
Trailheads

17

To Rochford, SD

85

To Newcastle, WY

10 Crow Peak Trail

A full-day hike winding upwards through pine forests to fantastic panoramas at the summit.

Start: Higgins Gulch Road (Forest Road 214), 6.9 miles west of Spearfish.
Distance: 7 miles out and back.
Approximate hiking time: Plan on a full day.
Difficulty: Moderately strenuous to strenuous.
Elevation gain: 1,560 feet.
Highest elevation: 5,760 feet.
Season: Late spring through fall.
Other trail users: Horses.
Land status: Black Hills National Forest.

Fees and permits: N/A
Maps: Black Hills National Forest Map; USDA Forest Service Crow Peak Trail Map No. 64 and Black Hills National Forest handout of Spearfish Trails, available free at area Forest Service offices and visitor centers.
Trail contact: Northern Hills Ranger District, 2014 North Main, Spearfish, SD 57783; (605) 642-4622.

Finding the trailhead: The trailhead is 6.9 miles west of Spearfish off Interstate 90 via exit 10. Take Utah Street (1 block east of the Forest Service office) west for 2.6 miles past a four-way stop sign. Take a left on Higgins Gulch Road (FR 214, a good gravel road) and follow it for 3.9 miles to the trailhead and a large parking area, on the right.

The Hike

Crow Peak Trail is a popular hike. The trail winds up to the mountaintop, providing sweeping vistas at the summit. Crow Peak is so named because of a battle once fought here between the Crow and Sioux Indians. Appropriately, the mountain in Sioux tongue, Paha Karitukateyapi, translates to "the place where the Sioux killed the Crow."

Crow Peak is an igneous intrusion and was formed in the same manner as Bear Butte and several other peaks in the area. Eons ago molten magma filled limestone and sedimentary layers, which then cooled to form the hard igneous rock. Erosion and washing away of sedimentary deposits continues to re-form the hills in the area.

The trail begins in Higgins Gulch amidst ponderosa-pine woods and much new growth of native bushes and bur oak. The 3.5 miles up the peak are moderate in some places, strenuous in others. The route heads west on the southern side of the hill and climbs ever upward. The trail is well blazed on trees with one large rectangle directly below a smaller rectangle.

At about 1.5 miles hikers encounter a junction. Here you might want to take the 1-mile round-trip Beaver Ridge Spur Trail to the south for more views in a peaceful atmosphere. If not, continue in a northerly direction toward the summit.

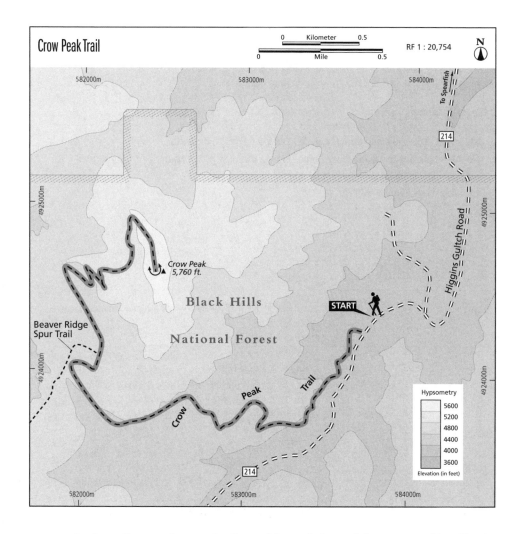

Crow Peak Trail

RF 1 : 20,754

0   Kilometer   0.5

0   Mile   0.5

N

To Spearfish

214

Higgins Gulch Road

Crow Peak
5,760 ft.

Black Hills

National Forest

START

Beaver Ridge
Spur Trail

Crow   Peak   Trail

214

Hypsometry

5600
5200
4800
4400
4000
3600

Elevation (in feet)

As the trail nears the top, the forest thins and the path becomes rockier. Simultaneously the trail offers the promise of spectacular views ahead—and at the peak lives up to its promise.

Our hike occurred on a mid-September day when several inches of early snow covered the peak. Where valleys retained pockets of cold, snow had lingered. At the summit the contrast between the valley and the peak was dramatic. Below, fall had barely tinged the trees, but several thousand feet higher, fall and winter were already colliding. The view from the top is almost surrealistic.

Lookout, Spearfish, and Terry Peaks as well as Bear Butte and other high points appear in the east. The plains of eastern Montana and the Bearlodge Mountains of Wyoming lie to the west, with Warren Peak sometimes visible. Spread below is the town of Spearfish, nestled in all this beauty.

Crow Peak Trail is designated for hikers and horsebackers only. The trail exhibits but little evidence of horse use and the typical erosion that often results from the tread of heavy animals is absent. Because the trail is steep, hikers might become dehydrated. Carry an ample supply of drinking water.

Miles and Directions

0.0 Start at the trailhead from the parking lot on Higgins Gulch Road.

1.5 The Spur Trail to Beaver Ridge comes in from the west (left). This out-and-back trail will add 1 mile to the hike if you elect to take it.

3.5 Backtrack from Crow Peak.

7.0 Return to the trailhead.

11 Old Baldy Trail

A mountain loop hike with a spur trail to the summit of Old Baldy, offering sweeping views of the northern Black Hills.

Start: At the trailhead on Tinton Road (Forest Road 134), about 13 miles south of Spearfish.
Distance: 7.7-mile loop with 2 stems (6.1 for loop only; 1.6 out and back on spur trail).
Approximate hiking time: Plan on nearly a full day.
Difficulty: Easy to moderate.
Highest elevation: 6,096 feet.
Seasons: Late spring through fall.

Other trail users: Horses.
Land status: Black Hills National Forest.
Fees and permits: N/A
Maps: Black Hills National Forest Map; Old Baldy Trail Map No. 66; USDA Black Hills National Forest handout, available free at area Forest Service offices and visitor centers.
Trail contact: Northern Hills Ranger District, 2014 North Main, Spearfish, SD 57783; (605) 642-4622.

Finding the trailhead: From Spearfish, take FR 134 (Tinton Road) south for 13 miles to the trailhead, on the right. Or take the Spearfish Canyon National Scenic Byway (U.S. Highway 14A) south from Spearfish for 12.8 miles to Savoy. At Savoy take Forest Road 222 (a good gravel road) south for 6 miles. Turn right on FR 134 and follow it for 1.2 miles to the trailhead on the left.

The trail also can be accessed (adding about 2 miles to the hike) by following the above directions to FR 222, then parking at the Little Spearfish trailhead, adjacent to Timon Campground. From here, hikers should take the Rimrock Trail Upper Loop north for 1 mile to a marker for Old Baldy Trail, near a quarry on the left. Another mile of hiking brings you to the trailhead and route described below.

Sunlight filters through the trees along
the trail to Old Baldy.

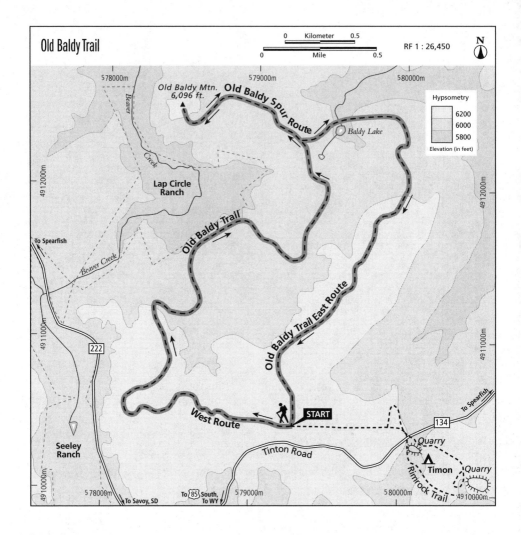

Old Baldy Trail

0 · Kilometer · 0.5
0 · Mile · 0.5

RF 1 : 26,450

N

578000m · 579000m · 580000m

Old Baldy Mtn.
6,096 ft.

Old Baldy Spur Route

Baldy Lake

Hypsometry

6200
6000
5800

Elevation (in feet)

Beaver

4912000m · 4912000m

Creek

**Lap Circle
Ranch**

Old Baldy Trail

To Spearfish

Beaver Creek

Old Baldy Trail East Route

4911000m · 4911000m

222

West Route

START

To Spearfish

134

Quarry

Seeley
Ranch

Tinton Road

Timon · Quarry

Rimrock Trail

4910000m · 4910000m

578000m · To Savoy, SD · To 85 South, To WY · 579000m · 580000m · 4910000m

The Hike

The Old Baldy Trail is a combination loop and spur trail that meanders through prime deer and elk habitat. Throughout the hike the trail is exceptionally well marked. Blazes are abundant and the grade is gentle. The trail could make for an ideal family outing, particularly for those interested in the possibility of observing wildlife. From Old Baldy Mountain, the vistas are satisfying, offering views to the east of Ragged Top and Terry Peak; to the west hikers can view Cement Ridge Lookout. Crow Peak looms in the north, a mountain with a geological background similar to that of Old Baldy.

The Old Baldy Trail, if followed along the western route, begins in a beautiful grove of aspens that includes much parklike terrain. The combination, with its understory of buckthorn *(Ceanothus)*, provides ideal winter habitat for elk, whose tracks and droppings are often abundant. For backpackers, numerous campsites exist because the terrain is relatively flat.

About 1 mile from the trailhead, the path descends gently and progresses north, crossing a broad bench. The trail then proceeds northwesterly for another 1.5 miles, paralleling the fence line of the Lap Circle Ranch. The trail swings southeast and ascends several hundred feet to a small bench where it then turns to the north.

The trail intersects with the Old Baldy Spur 1 mile later and then ascends 0.8 mile to the summit. The ascent is gentle and the climb can be completed quickly. Though Old Baldy Mountain is little more than a knob, the views are sweeping and encompass much of the Black Hills foothills as well as the peaks mentioned above. Botanically, the peak itself is classified as a dry-site environment, for the vegetation consists of ponderosa pine overlying an understory of mountain balm and some Oregon grape.

Retracing the 0.8-mile spur to the intersection, the return trip to the trailhead is but 2.6 miles. From the intersection, within 0.25 mile, the trail passes a small "lake" called Baldy Lake, created by a man-made dike. The resulting pond serves as a water hole for cattle, but judging from the abundant deer tracks, it also serves wildlife. The country here consists of open parklike areas and again provides ideal habitat for ungulates.

Shortly after passing Baldy Lake, the trail veers south and ascends via a series of gentle switchbacks to a small knob almost as high as Old Baldy. About 2.3 miles later the route concludes at the trailhead.

Miles and Directions

0.0 Start at the trailhead on Tinton Road.

2.5 The trail parallels the fence line at Lap Circle Ranch.

3.5 You've reached the Old Baldy Spur junction.

4.3 This is the Old Baldy summit.

5.1 You're back at the Old Baldy Spur junction.

5.4 Pass Old Baldy Lake.

7.7 Return to the trailhead.

12 Little Spearfish Trail

A three- to five-hour loop hike that rambles through ponderosa-pine forest and ends near a great walk-in fishing area.

Start: From the north side of Timon Campground off Forest Road 222; about 16 miles south of Spearfish.
Distance: 5.7-mile loop.
Approximate hiking time: 4 to 5 hours.
Difficulty: Moderate to easy.
Highest elevation: 6,280 feet.
Seasons: Late spring through fall.
Other trail users: Horses.
Land status: Black Hills National Forest.

Fees and permits: N/A
Maps: Black Hills National Forest Map; Little Spearfish Trail Map No. 80 and a free Black Hills National Forest handout, available at nearby Forest Service offices and visitor centers.
Trail contact: Northern Hills Ranger District, 2014 North Main, Spearfish, SD 57783; (605) 642-4622.

Finding the trailhead: Take U.S. Highway 14A (Spearfish Canyon National Scenic Byway) south from Spearfish for 12.8 miles to Savoy, or take US 14A northwest from Cheyenne Crossing (the southern terminus of the scenic byway) for 5.7 miles to Savoy. Then follow FR 222 south about 4 miles to the north side of Timon Campground, where the main trailhead is located. The trail can also be accessed from several points along FR 222 (signs are posted along the way).

The Hike

Beginning at Little Spearfish trailhead adjacent to Timon Campground, the trail proceeds east in the woods, paralleling FR 222 for about 0.8 mile. Cross the road twice, and at the second crossing pick up the trail again about 10 yards to the right.

Soon the trail heads south, still in the woods, into a moderately steep ascent that soon becomes a gentle climb until you reach the highest elevation of 6,280 feet. The ponderosa pines here are quite tall and not crowded. The trail is well worn through this lush setting, which is perfect elk and deer habitat.

About 3 miles from the start, the trail levels and swings sharply west/northwest. At this point, hikers encounter a dirt road and wire fence. Stay to the north (right) of the fence and look for blazes on the trees. Often the blazes are difficult to see, since they are cut into the tree bark. The next mile of trail descends through more elk and deer habitat.

The final mile, which is flat, wanders through meadows along Little Spearfish Creek and the walk-in fishing area. Those who like to fish will want to pack in a pole (and South Dakota license), since the trout are often visible in the abundant pools.

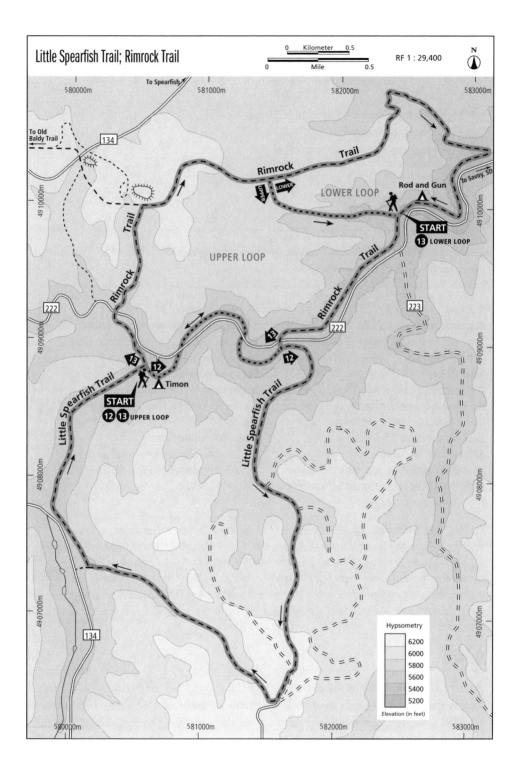

Little Spearfish Trail; Rimrock Trail

RF 1 : 29,400

N

Kilometer   0.5
Mile   0.5

To Spearfish

To Old
Baldy Trail

134

Rimrock   Trail

Rimrock

LOWER LOOP

UPPER

LOWER

Rod and Gun

To Savoy, SD

START

13 LOWER LOOP

UPPER LOOP

Rimrock

Trail

222

223

13

12

12

13

13

12

Timon

START

12 13 UPPER LOOP

Little Spearfish Trail

Little Spearfish Trail

134

Hypsometry

6200
6000
5800
5600
5400
5200

Elevation (in feet)

Miles and Directions

0.0 Start at the trailhead at Timon Campground, and travel east, paralleling FR 222.

0.8 Cross FR 222.

1.2 Ascend to the highest elevation, at 6,280 feet.

3.2 Trail swings northwest.

5.7 Return to the trailhead.

13 Rimrock Trail

Two loops or a combined circuit hike through large stands of ponderosa, aspen, and birch, with views of limestone cliffs.

See map on page 53

Start: At Timon Campground for the upper loop, and for easiest access to the lower loop, at the Rod and Gun Campground on Forest Road 222.

Distance: Upper Loop, 4.5 miles; Lower Loop, 3.5 miles. Eliminate the common middle section and hike the outer segments of both loops for a total of 6.5 miles.

Approximate hiking time: One-half day to a full day, depending on your choice of routes.

Difficulty: Upper Loop, moderately strenuous; Lower Loop, moderate.

Highest elevation: 6,040 feet.

Seasons: Best from late spring through fall.

Other trail users: Horses, mountain bikers.

Land status: Black Hills National Forest.

Fees and permits: N/A

Maps: Black Hills National Forest Map; Forest Service Rimrock Trail No. 79 Map available free from Forest Service offices, trailhead boxes, and visitor centers.

Trail contact: Northern Hills Ranger District, 2014 North Main, Spearfish, SD 57783; (605) 642–4622.

Finding the trailhead: Take U.S. Highway 14A (Spearfish Canyon National Scenic Byway) south from Spearfish for 12.8 miles to Savoy, or take US 14A northwest from Cheyenne Crossing (the southern terminus of the scenic byway) for 5.7 miles to Savoy. Then follow FR 222 south about 4 miles to the north side of Timon Campground, where the main trailhead is located. The trail can also be accessed from several points along FR 222 (signs are posted along the way). Rod and Gun Campground is 2 miles northeast on FR 222, offering access to both loops of the Rimrock Trail.

The Hike

To hike the **Upper Loop,** depart from the Little Spearfish trailhead (adjacent to Timon Campground) and make an initial climb to the north for about 100 yards. The ascent is quite steep and strenuous at first, then levels off to a gradual climb as the trail angles through the woods.

After 0.75 mile the junction for Old Baldy Trail to the west is encountered near the site of an old rock quarry. You've reached the maximum elevation now of 6,040 feet, and here the Rimrock Trail levels out, heading north and east.

More trail junctions occur in another 0.75 mile. To complete the Upper Loop, take the right fork, following the sign for the Rod and Gun Campground, reached in 1 mile. Again, turn right. At this point, about 2 miles remain to the trailhead, all of it level hiking that parallels bubbling Little Spearfish Creek, as well as FR 222. Along the route you'll see part of an old ranger station foundation and an old stone root cellar. The trail crosses the road three times before concluding back at Timon Campground.

The **Lower Loop** is the shorter of the two loop trails. To take this route, begin your hike at the Rod and Gun Campground. The trail begins at the west end of the campground, passes through a cattle gate, then ascends immediately for about 0.8 mile to the rim of the canyon, in a westerly direction. As you turn right (east), it then levels out through ponderosa pine, quaking aspen, and stands of birch for about 0.5 mile. Deer tracks abound, and flickers dart among the tree branches. The variation and abundance of plant life in this area is amazing and includes juniper, sage, varied wildflowers, buck brush, and kinnikinnick, a favorite grouse dish. The remainder of the trail provides a gradual descent into the depths of Little Spearfish Canyon, where the rock walls and formations stand in mute testimony to the forces of nature. A brief hike through tall grasses returns hikers to the trailhead.

The combined loops of the Rimrock Trail are designed for hikers, horsebackers, and mountain bikers. Horse use appears light, with no evidence of trail erosion.

Miles and Directions

Upper Loop

0.0 Start at Little Spearfish trailhead at Timon Campground.

0.75 The Old Baldy Trail comes in from the west; remain on the loop trail, which goes right (east).

1.5 Turn right (southeast) toward the Rod and Gun Campground.

2.5 You'll see a ranger station; turn right (south, then west).

4.5 Return to the trailhead.

Lower Loop

0.0 Start at the trailhead at Rod and Gun Campground.

0.8 You'll reach the canyon rim.

1.0 Trail intersection at a T. Go right (east).

3.5 Continue to the trailhead.

14 Big Hill Trails

A connecting series of trails at the summit of Big Hill, taking hikers through beautiful stands of quaking aspen, paper birch, and ponderosa pine and past sporadic views of the surrounding area.

Start: From Tinton Road (Forest Road 134) to Big Hill, about 9 miles from Spearfish.
Distance: Loops of various lengths, covering a total of 16.5 miles.
Approximate hiking time: A ½-hour to half a day to sample some loops.
Difficulty: Easy to moderate.
Highest elevation: 5,400 feet.
Seasons: Best from spring through winter, the fall being a perfect time.
Other trail users: Bikers, horses, and cross-country skiers.

Land status: Black Hills National Forest.
Fees and permits: N/A
Maps: Black Hills National Forest Map; Big Hill Trail Map No. 72; a free Black Hills National Forest handout is available at area Forest Service offices, the trailhead box, or nearby visitor centers.
Trail contact: Northern Hills Ranger District, 2014 North Main, Spearfish, SD 57783; (605) 642-4622.

Finding the trailhead: From Spearfish, take Jackson Boulevard, which crosses Main Street in the center of town, southwest to the top of the hill. Follow signs to the left for Tinton Road (FR 134), which is a good gravel road. Follow FR 134 for 7.8 miles to the top of Big Hill and the small parking lot on the right, which has a sign for Big Hill Trails. The trailheads are directly across the road.

The Hike

Fall is a perfect time to hike the many trails of this area as gold aspens and birches shimmer against the dark green ponderosa pines. Early in the morning, families of deer still browse and coyotes howl across the ridgetops. This is prime elk habitat, too.

This is rolling country, with the trails following the gentle slopes. All trails wander through the mixed stands of trees in the woods. Atop Big Hill solitude abounds and offers hikers a chance to enjoy the peace and a variety of views. According to the Forest Service handout, Big Hill was so named long ago by miners heading south from Spearfish to the goldfields. With all the wagons and teams, it was a real grind to make it over the big hill.

We sampled the area's trails by combining Loops A and B into one hike of about 3 miles. To access the loops, walk southeast a brief 0.25 mile to where Loop A begins; taking the left fork brings you to Loop C, which runs to the rim of Spearfish Canyon, 1,000 feet deep. The right fork takes hikers to Loop B or C. Loop D is reached from the southern part of Loop C. Loop A is the shortest route at 2.1 miles, and Loop C is the longest at 5.5 miles.

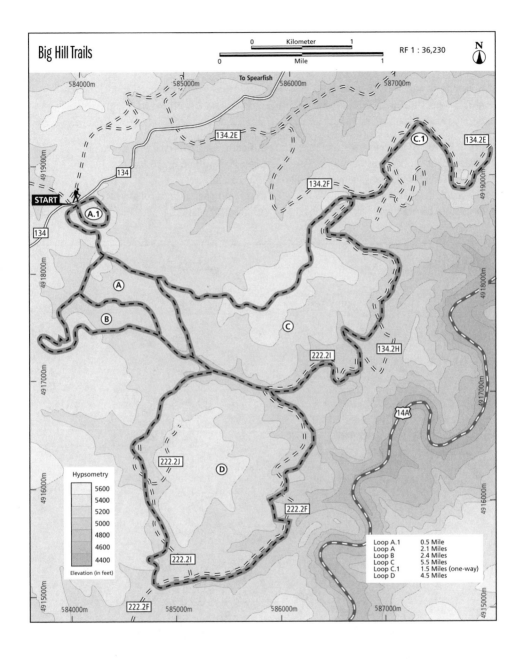

Big Hill Trails

RF 1 : 36,230

N

0 Kilometer 1
0 Mile 1

To Spearfish

134.2E

C.1

134.2E

134

134.2F

START

A.1

134

A

B

C

134.2H

222.2I

14A

222.2J

D

Hypsometry

5600
5400
5200
5000
4800
4600
4400

Elevation (in feet)

222.2F

Loop A.1	0.5 Mile
Loop A	2.1 Miles
Loop B	2.4 Miles
Loop C	5.5 Miles
Loop C.1	1.5 Miles (one-way)
Loop D	4.5 Miles

222.2I

222.2F

Big Hill Trails are designed for hikers, bikers, horsebackers, and cross-country skiers, and the area is designated "multiple use." The trails and loops are well marked with signposts and tree blazes.

15 Eagle Cliff Trails

An extensive series of twenty loop and one-way trails, originally designed for cross-country skiers but also used by hikers, mountain bikers, and horseback riders.

Start: From one of two trailheads off U.S. Highway 85, about 30 miles from Spearfish.
Distance: Various trails, ranging from 0.2 mile to 3.4 miles, in many combinations.
Approximate hiking time: 1 hour to a full day.

Difficulty: Easy to moderately strenuous.
Highest elevation: 6,250 feet.
Seasons: All.
Other trail users: Cross-country skiers, mountain bikers, horses.

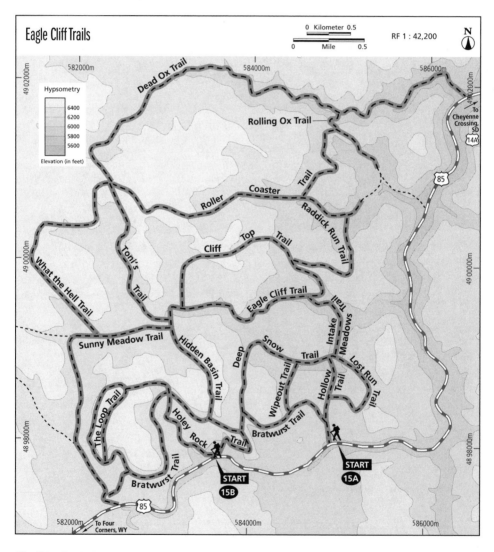

Land status: Black Hills National Forest.

Fees and permits: N/A

Maps: Black Hills National Forest Map; Eagle Cliff Trail Map No. 68; free Black Hills National Forest handout, available at area Forest Service offices and visitor centers.

Trail contact: Northern Hills Ranger District, 2014 North Main, Spearfish, SD 57783; (605) 642-4622.

Finding the trailheads: From Spearfish, take U.S. Highway 14A (a National Scenic Byway) south for 22 miles to Cheyenne Crossing. Then take US 85 south for 7.4 miles to the first trailhead (A), or 8.4 miles to the second trailhead (B). Both trailheads are north of the highway.

The Hike

This rugged, high, somewhat remote series of loop trails offers short trips of an hour or the opportunity to hike for several days. Many loop combinations are possible, and ambitious hikers may want to try one long perimeter hike. Unique trail names such as What the Hell, Wipe Out, and Deep Snow reflect the fact that local cross-country skiers began this system.

Additional Hikes

Hikers may enjoy several other short hikes in the Spearfish area. Among them are the following:

Mount Roosevelt

A trail up Mount Roosevelt goes 0.5 mile one-way to the top. Hikers can rest at the overlooks of Mount Roosevelt as the trail winds through stands of aspen and large boulders, offering grand views along the way and at the summit. The trail is an easy one, with an elevation gain of 150 feet and a maximum elevation of 5,600 feet.

The Mount Roosevelt trail makes a fun, easy jaunt for the entire family. The elevation gain is minimal, the views are nice, and the trail is a good one. Historic Friendship Tower atop the mountain was built by Seth Bullock, a Deadwood rancher, as a tribute to his deep friendship with President Theodore Roosevelt.

Mount Roosevelt is located a short distance northwest of Deadwood, South Dakota. To find the trailhead, take U.S. Highway 85 south from Interstate 90, just east of Spearfish. US 85 is well marked from I–90. Just before reaching the town of Deadwood, take Forest Road 133 west from US 85. Go approximately 3 miles and park in the lot at the picnic area.

Roughlock Falls

The Savoy area is a popular one for several reasons. Here, two huge canyons, Spearfish and Little Spearfish, come together to offer spectacular views. The ancient rock formations are a geologist's delight. And Little Spearfish Canyon offers wonderful hiking trails and fishing spots.

The trail to Roughlock Falls is a flat, 1-mile walk along Spearfish Creek to the picturesque waterfall, which is a favorite picnic spot. The trail is easy and barrier-free, accessible to visitors in wheelchairs. The cascading falls are charming at all times of the year. The falls are so named because, before the current road existed, the old wagon and log-sled path was very steep. Drivers "rough-locked" the wheels of their vehicles with ropes or chains so the wagons would drag instead of jacking out of control.

Roughlock Falls are located about 0.5 mile from Savoy on Forest Road 222. To reach Savoy, take U.S. Highway 14A (Spearfish Canyon National Scenic Byway) south from Spearfish for 12.8 miles. Drive about 0.5 mile south of Savoy on FR 222 to a parking area on your left. From here, you can hike a wide, tree-lined path for 1 mile along Spearfish Creek to Roughlock Falls.

Custer State Park

In 1919, through the mighty efforts of South Dakota governor Peter Norbeck and others, land that once had been a state game preserve became Custer State Park. Today the park contains 71,000 acres consisting of grasslands, ponderosa-pine forests, bur oak, and white spruce. As a wildlife preserve, Custer has one of the world's largest bison herds and is home to elk, deer, bighorn sheep, and even mountain goats. Custer is also one of the largest state parks in our nation. Appropriately, the park serves as an excellent area for recreation, offering trout fishing in its many streams and man-made lakes.

The park offers abundant camping spots and trails for hikers, which encompass the area's grasslands and the forest areas. Though the trail system is not extensive, it is varied. Trails in Custer State Park wind through prairies, mountains, and incredible

At one time bison in North America exceeded 30 million head. Today bison still thunder across the prairies and grasslands in Custer State Park.

Custer State Park Overview

rock formations. They offer abundant views of wildlife, lakes, and streams. They're varied enough to let you hear the insects, to see the abundant wildlife, and to allow winds to shape your thoughts.

When hiking in Custer State Park, always be aware of the possibility of bison encounters. Never approach these huge, shaggy monarchs. A cow with her calf in the spring represents a threat, as do animals of both sexes in the mating season in July and August.

For the adventurer in search of a vignette of primitive America, a South Dakota that once was, few places offer better examples than the Black Hills. Though summer and fall are ideal times to hike here, we recommend fall as the best season. The days are cool, and the aspen, birch, and bur oak assume colors that reflect the presence of plant pigments beyond the usual green chlorophyll.

The bighorn sheep population in Custer State Park numbers about 150 to 200.

Custer State Park is located in the southeast portion of the Black Hills, directly north of Wind Cave National Park and about a 30-minute drive south from Rapid City, South Dakota. From Interstate 90 at Rapid City, take South Dakota Highway 79 south for 17 miles. About 1 mile south of the town of Hermosa, follow South Dakota Highway 36 west for 9 miles to U.S. Highway 16A west, which will take you to the park's east entrance.

For an alternative scenic route, drive through the center of the Black Hills. To do so, proceed from Spearfish off I–90, taking U.S. Highway 85 south to U.S. Highway 385 south. Take US 16A east at the town of Custer into Custer State Park. If you are heading west, take I–90 west to Sturgis, then take U.S. Highway 14 west toward Deadwood. Take US 385 south, following the above suggestions from Spearfish. State highway maps show the numerous cutoffs to these routes, and signs pointing the way to Custer State Park can be found throughout the Black Hills.

Two visitor centers exist in the park. The Peter Norbeck Visitor Center is located on the park's main road (US 16A) about 3 miles west of the junction of SD 36 and US 16A; it is open from April through November. The Wildlife Station Visitor

Center is located on the eastern portion of the Wildlife Loop Road and is open from the end of May through September.

To become acquainted with the park and its multitudinous offerings, we found it helpful as well as rewarding to drive all three of the scenic roads provided to visitors. The vistas are incredible, and for those planning to hike, the drives furnish a good overview of trail locations (see overview map for road locations). The drives take longer than the mileages indicate because the roads are winding. The Needles Highway is 14 miles long and curves its way around magnificent granite formations. The Iron Mountain Road is 16 miles in length, with pigtail bridges and tunnels carved from the granite rock. This road leads from the park to Mount Rushmore. The 18-mile Wildlife Loop Road shows another side of the park—its rolling prairie grasslands and their magnificent display of wildlife.

A small day-use fee is charged for spending time in Custer State Park.

16 The Creekside Trail

A beautiful stroll on a hard-surface path that parallels Grace Coolidge Creek. This path is available to walkers, bikers, and those with in-line skates; it is also wheelchair accessible.

See map on page 66
Start: From any location along the path, which runs from Game Lodge Campground to Grace Coolidge Campground.

Distance: Up to 4 miles out and back.
Difficulty: Easy.
Land status: Custer State Park.
Fees and permits: Park fee.

Finding the trailhead: Begin at the State Game Lodge Campground on the Wildlife Loop Road or at Grace Coolidge Campground. The trail runs between these two campgrounds and parallel to US 16A.

The Hike

This recently established trail follows Grace Coolidge Creek and passes by the historic Game Lodge, the Peter Norbeck Visitor Center, Coolidge General Store, and the Park Office. You may access the trail at any of these locations.

17 French Creek Natural Area

An overnight backpack or a long day hike into a pristine natural area along a gorge of unique rock formations, with numerous creek fordings. Of course, you always have the option of hiking in from either end and backtracking when you get tired.

Start: From either the west end of the French Creek Trail on Custer State Park Road 4 or the east end on the Wildlife Loop Road.
Distance: 12 miles one-way.
Approximate hiking time: An overnight trip or a full-day trip to complete the 12 miles.
Difficulty: Moderate.
Seasons: Best in late spring through fall.
Other trail users: Horseback riders.

Land status: Custer State Park.
Fees and permits: Park fee; campers must self-register at either trailhead.
Maps: National Geographic/Trails Illustrated Topo Map No. 238; free Custer State Park Trail Guide, available at park visitor centers and entrances.
Trail contact: Custer State Park, HC 83, Box 70, Custer, SD 57730; (605) 255-4515.

Finding the trailhead: To access the east trailhead, head east from Peter Norbeck Visitor Center on U.S. Highway 16A. Go 0.8 mile to the Wildlife Loop Road, on the right. Turn right and follow this road south for 4 miles to the trailhead sign on the right.

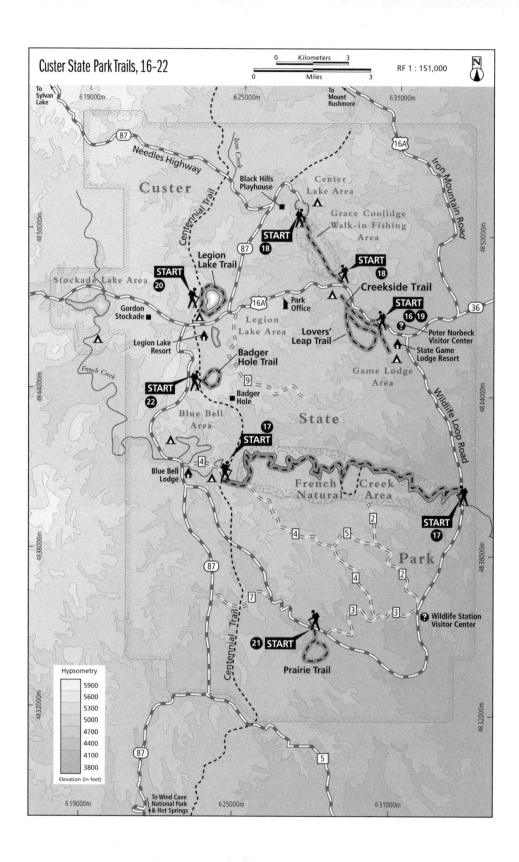

Custer State Park Trails, 16–22

Kilometers
0   3
0   3
Miles

RF 1 : 151,000

N

To Sylvan Lake
619000m
625000m
To Mount Rushmore
631000m

87
Needles Highway
Iron Creek
16A
Iron Mountain Road

Custer
Black Hills Playhouse
Center Lake Area
Grace Coolidge Walk-in Fishing Area

4850000m
Centennial Trail
START 18
87
START 18
Creekside Trail
36

Legion Lake Trail
16A
Park Office
START 16 19
?
Peter Norbeck Visitor Center

START 20
Stockade Lake Area
Legion Lake Area
Lovers' Leap Trail
State Game Lodge Resort
Gordon Stockade
Legion Lake Resort
Game Lodge Area

French Creek
Badger Hole Trail
9

4844000m
START 22
Badger Hole
State
Wildlife Loop Road

Blue Bell Area
START 17
4

Blue Bell Lodge
French Creek Natural Area
START 17

87
4
5
2
Park
4848000m→ 4838000m

2
4
2

7
3
3
Wildlife Station Visitor Center

Centennial Trail
21 START
Prairie Trail

Hypsometry
5900
5600
5300
5000
4700
4400
4100
3800
Elevation (in feet)

4832000m

87
5

619000m
To Wind Cave National Park & Hot Springs
625000m
631000m

Watch your step at this stream crossing in the French Creek Natural Area.

To reach the west trailhead, continue south on Wildlife Loop Road to Blue Bell Lodge, a total of 20 miles. From here, take Custer State Park Road 4 (gravel) east for 3 miles to the trailhead. Parking is available at both trailheads.

The Hike

French Creek originates northwest of the town of Custer. It feeds Stockade Lake and continues its eastward flow, passing through Custer State Park and into the 2,200-acre French Creek Natural Area. The creek cuts into the land in a dramatic manner.

Over its next 12 miles, the creek exposes some of the Black Hills' most spectacular granitic and sedimentary layers in the form of narrow defiles and cozy, colorful canyons. Surrounding walls rise boldly and radiate colors of red, orange, and yellow.

Near here, at the present site of the Gordon Stockade, a member of Lt. Col. George Armstrong Custer's 1874 expedition to the Black Hills discovered gold, a presence that was to alter treaties and revise forever the interaction of native peoples and settlers here.

For the angler/hiker the French Creek area offers some of the state's best fishing. Brown and rainbow trout in the canyon's deep holes and numerous riffles respond well to dry flies and spinners. For the nature hiker the canyons offer abundant wildlife sightings in the form of turkey, deer, elk, and bands of bighorn sheep. In fall, bull elk lift their heads and bugle, and the canyon's walls ring to the sonorous cry of wandering males attempting to proclaim their territories and establish harems.

Here, too, is a geological phenomenon. Near the eastern end of the natural area, waters in French Creek disappear in dry times over a several-hundred-yard span of stream. Geologists call this phenomenon sinkhole topography, saying that in the distant millennia, subsurface pockets were formed where soft sedimentary rock was engulfed by harder sedimentary rock. Eventually the soft rock eroded. The void was filled, in this case, by French Creek, particularly noticeable in the drier season. But about 1 mile in from the eastern trailhead, the creek ceases in a very dramatic fashion: Now you see it, now you don't.

French Creek Natural Area offers camping sites anywhere along the trail, but open fires are *not allowed*. From either trailhead, the path is a well-traveled one, but sometimes you must create your own trails or follow those left by others. In one section of the French Creek hike, about 5 miles in from the eastern trailhead, hikers are challenged by sheer rock walls in a place called the Narrows. Since there is no place to walk, a swim or a very steep ascent around it is in order. But you'll never get lost if you simply follow the stream.

Paths generally parallel the creek until they approach the trail's western terminus some 10 miles later. Hikers in French Creek are cautioned about the hazards of the area: Maintain a watchful eye for bison and rattlesnakes, be aware of the abundance of poison ivy, and know in advance that you'll have about thirty-four creek crossings.

Miles and Directions

0.0 Start at the eastern terminus, on the Wildlife Loop Road.

0.5 The stream disappears.

5.0 Sheer rock walls challenge hikers.

12.0 End the hike at the western terminus.

18 Grace Coolidge Walk-in Fishing Area

A beautiful, fairly flat walk terminating or beginning at Grace Coolidge Campground or Center Lake, paralleling (with many crossings) Grace Coolidge Creek. Good fishing abounds here.

See map on page 66
Start: From either Grace Coolidge Campground or Center Lake.
Distance: 5.6 miles out and back.
Approximate hiking time: 4 to 6 hours.
Difficulty: Easy.
Seasons: Best from midspring through fall.
Other trail users: Bikers.
Land status: Custer State Park.

Fees and permits: Park fee. A fishing license is required if you plan to fish.
Maps: National Geographic/Trails Illustrated Topo Map No. 238; free Custer State Park Trail Guide available at visitor centers and entrance stations.
Trail contact: Custer State Park, HC 83, Box 70, Custer, SD 57730; (605) 255-4515.

Finding the trailhead: To find the southern trailhead, take U.S. Highway 16A west from the Peter Norbeck Visitor Center for 1.5 miles. The trailhead is on the right, across the road from the Grace Coolidge Campground.

To access the northern trailhead, take US 16A west from visitor center to South Dakota Highway 87 north. Go 8 miles to the turnoff for Center Lake and the Black Hills Playhouse, then go in 1 mile to Center Lake. The trailhead is located by the shower house above the lake.

The Hike

The Grace Coolidge Walk-in Fishing Area trail is actually an old, overgrown logging road. It is an easy and refreshing hike, and the numerous crossings over the narrow, sometimes deep, creek add to the fun. Six low-head dams exist along the way, some with deep, dark pools lying beneath granite rock formations. Walking this trail is a fun outing for the entire family. In 1927 President Calvin Coolidge and his family maintained a summer White House nearby; as a result, many features in the area bear the Coolidge name.

In summer the trail is alive with the vibrant colors of wildflowers; in fall the bur oak and birch tree leaves add a startling gold that contrasts with the green-black of the ponderosa pine. As in many low, wet areas, poison ivy is abundant along the trail and by the creek.

Photo opportunities abound here, as do chances for excellent fishing. The pools are stocked with brook and rainbow trout, so hiking anglers should be sure to pack in fishing gear along with their South Dakota license.

Miles and Directions

0.0 Start at the trailhead across the road from the Grace Coolidge Campground (southern trailhead).

1.4 Granite rock formations.

2.8 Arrive at the northern trailhead at Center Lake.

5.6 Turn around and retrace your steps to the southern trailhead.

19 Lovers' Leap Trail

A two- to three-hour loop trail passing through a ponderosa-pine and oak forest, offering great views at the summit. There are many creek crossings (and no bridges).

See map on page 66
Start: From the trailhead behind the schoolhouse across from the Peter Norbeck Visitor Center on U.S. Highway 16A.
Distance: A 3-mile loop.
Approximate hiking time: 2 to 3 hours.
Difficulty: Moderately strenuous for the first 30 minutes, then moderate to easy.
Highest elevation: 4,780 feet.
Seasons: Best late spring through fall.

Other trail users: Hikers only.
Land status: Custer State Park.
Fees and permits: Park fee.
Maps: National Geographic/Trails Illustrated Topo Map No. 238; free Custer State Park Trail Guide booklet available at the park office, visitor centers, and entrances.
Trail contact: Custer State Park, HC 83, Box 70, Custer, SD 57730; (605) 255-4515.

Finding the trailhead: The trail begins behind the schoolhouse across from the Peter Norbeck Visitor Center on US 16A, which is 3 miles east of the park entrance station off South Dakota Highway 36.

The Hike

With lots of potential for a fun family outing, this popular hike combines gentle ups and downs after an initial steep ascent to a ridge; numerous stream crossings exist, though none is too difficult. Hikers should remain alert for poison ivy, which is abundant near the streams.

According to legend, Lovers' Leap derives its name from a Native American couple who elected to end their lives by plummeting from the lofty outcropping of rocks on a 200-foot ridge. Just why the couple leaped to their deaths is not remembered. Today a lone ponderosa pine stands among the conglomerate rocks overlooking the sheer drop of several hundred feet. Not surprisingly, the ridge commands spectacular views of the Black Hills.

The overlook is reached by following the broad trail from the schoolhouse where it immediately begins a thirty- to forty-five-minute, relatively steep climb

This is just one of ten stream crossings along Lovers' Leap Trail.

through bur oak and ponderosa-pine forest. Prairie grasses mat the hillsides as you climb to the top. As you approach the summit, interesting rock formations and lichen-covered boulders are scattered on the hill to your right.

At the trail's highest point, a sign greets you and provides the following message: "Custer State Park is a place where one can still be an unworried and unregimented individual and wear any old clothes and sit on a log and get his sanity back again." Beyond the trail and sign, hikers can climb the short distance through the boulders and reach the deadly "lovers' leap" point.

The view from the summit (elevation 4,780 feet) is spectacular. Across the valley and in the near distance are the charred remains of the Galena Fire of 1988. Looking beyond, on clear days, hikers are treated to a view of Harney Peak, Mount Coolidge, and the Cathedral Spires.

Upon leaving Lovers' Leap, the trail descends the west side of the ridge to Galena Creek, and here hikers may experience some difficulty. The trail meanders along the narrow creek bed and makes ten stream crossings. In dry times, crossing is easy, but in wet years the water remains high. Poison ivy abounds along the creek bed and the trail, so wear long pants and watch where you place your feet. Much of the trail is flanked with less irritating, lovelier wildflowers such as sedum, highbush cranberry, cow parsnip, Bicknell's geranium, mountain meadowsweet, bluebells, salsify, and many prairie grasses.

After the last stream crossing, the trail leads to a gravel road and passes by the Coolidge Inn. A ten-minute walk will return you to the schoolhouse and the trailhead.

Miles and Directions

0.0 Start at the trailhead behind the schoolhouse across from the visitor center on US 16A.

2.0 Climb to the Lovers' Leap Overlook.

2.5 A series of stream crossings begins.

3.0 Return to the trailhead.

20 Legion Lake Trail

A pleasant 1½-hour loop hike that climbs a hill on the north side of Legion Lake and offers views of the surrounding area.

See map on page 66
Start: From the trailhead in Legion Lake Campground, 6 miles west of Peter Norbeck Visitor Center.
Distance: 1.5-mile loop.
Approximate hiking time: 1 to 2 hours.
Difficulty: Moderate.
Seasons: Late spring through fall.
Other trail users: Horses, mountain bikers.

Land status: Custer State Park.
Fees and permits: Park fee.
Maps: National Geographic/Trails Illustrated Topo Map No. 238; free Custer State Park Trail Guide booklet available at park office, visitor centers, and entrances.
Trail contact: Custer State Park, HC 83, Box 70, Custer, SD 57730; (605) 255-4515.

Finding the trailhead: From the Peter Norbeck Visitor Center, take U.S. Highway 16A west for 6 miles to Legion Lake Campground, on the right. Drive to the far end of the campground, where the trailhead is clearly marked. Park in front of the shower house or across the highway. Please do not block the campsites.

The Hike

The Legion Lake Trail climbs counterclockwise through a ponderosa-pine forest, where hikers see evidence of timber thinning and management. The summit is reached after 0.75 mile. From its rocky outcroppings, hikers can view the lake below, the Badlands to the east, and the southern Black Hills. Toward the end of the 0.75-mile descent, Centennial Trail joins in from the north and completes the loop back to the campground.

Various species of mammals and birds use this area, including wandering bison. Please remember that bison can be dangerous.

Miles and Directions

0.0 Start at the trailhead at Legion Lake Campground

0.75 The saddle is reached.

1.1 Centennial Trail joins from the north.

1.5 Return to the trailhead.

21 Prairie Trail

An easy interpretive loop hike through prairie grasslands and over open ridges, with superb views.

See map on page 66
Start: At the well-marked trailhead on the Wildlife Loop Road.
Distance: 3-mile lollipop.
Approximate hiking time: 2 to 3 hours.
Difficulty: Moderate.
Seasons: Best late spring through fall.
Other trail users: Bikers, horses.

Land status: Custer State Park.
Fees and permits: Park fee.
Maps: National Geographic/Trails Illustrated Topo Map No. 238; free Custer State Park Trail Guide available at park office, visitor centers, and entrance stations.
Trail contact: Custer State Park, HC 83, Box 70, Custer, SD 57730; (605) 255-4515.

Finding the trailhead: From the Peter Norbeck Visitor Center on U.S. Highway 16A, go east for 0.8 mile to the Wildlife Loop Road intersecting from the south. Take a right onto the Wildlife Loop Road and follow it for approximately 14 miles. The well-marked trailhead is on the left, with a small parking area.

From the Blue Bell entrance station on South Dakota Highway 87, take the Wildlife Loop Road southeast for 5 miles to the trailhead on the right.

The Hike

The Prairie Trail was designed especially for those interested in viewing prairie grasslands and wildflowers. The interpretive signs along the way help ensure more correct interpretation and add to the enjoyment of the hike. The elevation gain is modest, climbing but 250 feet.

Views offered along this trail are commanding, and on a clear day, hikers are rewarded with distant views to the east of the White River Badlands. Even from afar, when the interplay of light and land is appropriate, the area appears majestic. So, too, does the grassland over which hikers must pass. Views of the prairie suggest an immensity and grandeur found in few other areas of the United States.

The flora is varied, and throughout the summer, pageants of flowers reward hikers. Alert travelers might also see and hear a variety of birds and mammals, such as mountain bluebirds, golden eagles, coyotes, and pronghorns.

The Prairie Trail begins by immediately crossing the narrow South Fork of Lame Johnny Creek, which, following rains, generally means wet feet. The path meanders through the grassland for a short distance, then ascends 0.25 mile along a relatively steep bluff through a stand of bur oak to a high plateau.

After breaking free from the trees, the trail follows this plateau of grasses and flowers, then descends to a fence used for bison management. The gate in the fence is your access to the trail. From here you descend a short distance along the trail to where you must ford Flynn Creek, which offers an excellent example of riparian habitat.

The trail ascends again, passing through stands of bur oak, the only oak indigenous to the Black Hills. As the trail reaches the next plateau, called Hay Flats, the path winds through stands of ponderosa pine on the edge of the flats. The trail follows the plateau, passing numerous bison wallows. Soon the trail encounters another bison fence, again with a gate provided. The fences divide the park into smaller pasturelike divisions so that the bison can be rotated among them, thus not overgrazing any one area. Near the end of the hike, you'll follow a small stream through stands of hardwoods; the trail is marked with posts and rock cairns.

About 3 miles out, the trail concludes where it began by Lame Johnny Creek.

Miles and Directions

0.0 Begin at the trailhead on Wildlife Loop Road. Cross creek.

0.25 Reach high plateau; join the loop here, walking clockwise.

0.75 Come to gate in fence.

0.85 Descend to Flynn Creek; cross.

1.0 Trail ascends to Hay Flats.

2.0 Come to second gate in fence.

2.75 Turn left off the loop back onto the stem to retrace your steps.

3.0 Return to the trailhead and the end of the hike.

22 Badger Clark Historic Trail

A short loop trail that winds behind the historic cabin of Charles Badger Clark (1883–1957), first poet laureate of South Dakota.

See map on page 66

Start: At the trailhead on Badger Hole Drive (Park Road 9) off U.S. Highway 16A.

Distance: A 1-mile loop.

Approximate hiking time: 1 to 2 hours.

Difficulty: Moderate.

Seasons: Spring through fall.

Other trail users: Hikers only.

Land status: Custer State Park.

Fees and permits: Custer State Park entry permit.

Maps: Free Custer State Park Trail Guide and interpretive booklet available at park office, visitor centers, and entrance stations.

Trail contact: Custer State Park, HC 83, Box 70, Custer, SD 57730; (605) 255-4515.

Finding the trailhead: From the Peter Norbeck Visitor Center, take US 16A west for 5.5 miles to the sign on the left for the Badger Hole (Park Road 9). Follow this road for 1 mile to Badger Hole Drive on the right. Turn right and go less than 0.1 mile to the trailhead parking lot.

The Hike

> There's a song in the canyon below me
> And a song in the pines overhead,
> As the sunlight crawls down from the snowline
> And rustles the deer from his bed.
> With mountains of green all around me
> And mountains of white up above
> And mountains of blue down the ski-line,
> I follow the trail that I love.
>
> —Badger Clark,
> in *The Old Prospector in Sun and Saddle Leather*

This short, historic interpretive walk is great for the entire family. The trail exists because the area was once the haunt of poet Badger Clark, best known perhaps for his poem "Cowboy's Prayer." Clark lived alone for thirty years in this pristine setting, inspired by nature's bounty. He first built a one-room cabin, where he lived for ten years while building a slightly larger cabin just up the hill. An interpretive trail brochure tells more about Clark's life and is available at the cabin and the park's visitor centers.

The trail begins with a moderate clockwise ascent through pine. At about 0.5 mile you can see the charred remains of the Galena Fire of 1988 and the lookout tower atop Mount Coolidge (6,023 feet). Note the large rocks placed along the trail as it ascends to the vista. According to the interpretive brochure, this was the area where Clark originally wanted to be buried, and so he began lining the path with rocks. He often traveled this path, which provided inspiration for his work.

Home of poet laureate Badger Clark, accessible by a short trail that then leads to sweeping views of the Black Hills.

Custer State Park has provided ten stops along the trail, with poetry selections to be read from the brochure at each stop. You'll also note that one of the three Centennial Trail trailheads in Custer State Park is located near this place known as the "Badger Hole."

23 Sunday Gulch Trail

An interpretive trail that loops behind Sylvan Lake and offers some of the best overviews of the park's exquisite diversity. This trail is closed in the winter.

Start: From the Sylvan Lake Shore Trail, going behind the dam to the Sunday Gulch Trail.
Distance: 2.8-mile loop.
Approximate hiking time: 2 to 3 hours.
Difficulty: Moderately strenuous to strenuous.
Seasons: Best from early June through fall; closed in winter.
Land status: Custer State Park.

Fees and permits: A Custer State Park entry permit.
Maps: National Geographic/Trails Illustrated Topo Map No. 238; free Custer State Park Trail Guide booklet available at park office, visitor centers, and entrances.
Trail contact: Custer State Park, HC 83, Box 70, Custer, SD 57730; (605) 255-4515.

Finding the trailhead: From Peter Norbeck Visitor Center, take U.S. Highway 16A west, then take South Dakota Highway 87 north then west to Sylvan Lake, a total distance of 18.8 miles. Park in the day-use parking lot. Walk the Sylvan Lake Shore Trail east for 0.25 mile to the trailhead sign on the left. Or come in at the Sylvan Lake entrance station via U.S. Highways 16/385 south from Hill City to SD 87 south to Sylvan Lake.

From Custer, take South Dakota Highway 89 north for approximately 7 miles to Sylvan Lake.

The Hike

The Sunday Gulch Trail is considered so extraordinary in its spectrum of plants, trees, mosses, and great scenery that it was designated a National Recreation Trail in 1971. You'll hike counterclockwise starting off to the northwest. This beautiful trail immediately descends steeply for 0.25 mile, winding over huge rocks as it drops into the depths of Sunday Gulch. The rocks can be slippery; some stone steps and

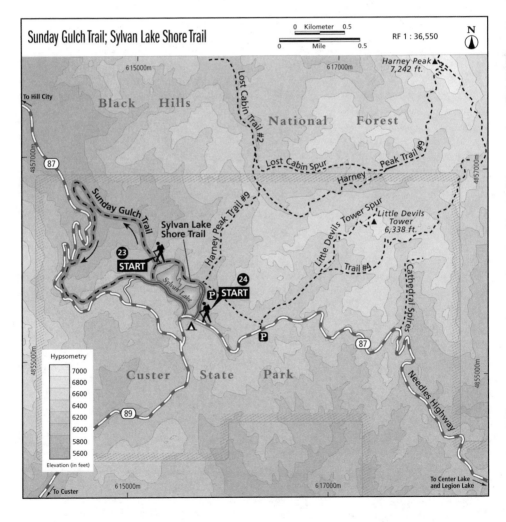

handrails are provided for the first portion of the hike. Exercise caution on this part of the descent, since sometimes the handrails have been loosened over the winter by ice pushing on the railings. Often the trail is still ice-packed in May.

As you begin the descent, huge granite walls tower on each side of the trail, which parallels the creek as it drops into the ravine. Various rock layers and formations exist here. Tiny waterfalls and rock grottos surrounded by ponderosa pine, Black Hills spruce (*Picea glauca* var. *densata*), paper birch, and aspen provide photo opportunities. Old man's beard, a gray-green lichen, hangs from the trees, adding to the mystery of the gulch. Many of the rocks are covered with mosses and lichen. Once this gulch was filled with a stream, but in the 1890s Theodor Reder dammed the mouth of the gulch and created Sylvan Lake. Today the stream spills over the dam, and at least one deep pool provides a home to brown trout.

As the trail ascends from the gulch, beautiful panoramas of the Needles formations slide into view. Toward trail's end hikers encounter a power line, and at times the trail parallels the road; still, the beauty of the area is not diminished. The trail is well marked with orange blazes on trees.

24 Sylvan Lake Shore Trail

An easy loop trail around the shore of beautiful Sylvan Lake.

See map on page 77
Start: At the Sylvan Lake Day-Use area off South Dakota Highway 87.
Distance: 1-mile loop.
Approximate hiking time: 1 hour.
Difficulty: Easy.
Seasons: All, but best from spring through fall.
Land status: Custer State Park.

Fees and permits: Custer State Park entry permit.
Maps: Free Custer State Park Trail Guide available at park office, visitor centers, and entrance stations.
Trail contact: Custer State Park, HC 83, Box 70, Custer, SD 57730; (605) 255-4515.

Finding the trailhead: From Peter Norbeck Visitor Center, take U.S. Highway 16A west to SD 87 north (Needles Highway) then west to Sylvan Lake Day-Use area, a total of 19 miles.

The Hike

The Sylvan Lake Shore Trail is an interpretive trail, one of the easiest in Custer State Park. This trail makes a loop around the lake, affording hikers wonderful views of the gigantic granite rocks in and around the lake. Feel free to walk in either direction. This extremely easy walk is for everyone. The majority of the trail is barrier-free, accessible to those in wheelchairs, but a small portion has steps and some rocky areas.

◀ *Lichen- and moss-covered boulders are part of the scenery on the Sunday Gulch Trail.*

Harney Range

To the Lakota of the Black Hills, Harney Peak is a mythical mountain. Black Elk, a prominent medicine man among the Oglala people, considered Harney Peak the center of the world. For him, it was a place for vision quests and spiritual rejuvenation. In addition to the mountain's spiritual embodiments, Harney Peak is a significant mountain because it is the highest peak east of the main chain of the Rocky Mountains.

Harney Peak's features enchant hikers who follow trails to the peak's 7,242-foot summit. From a historic lookout tower atop the summit, hikers have distant panoramic views of South Dakota, Nebraska, Wyoming, and Montana, as well as close-up vantage points of the granite formations and cliffs of the Black Elk Wilderness.

Harney Peak was named for General William S. Harney, the commanding officer of Lieutenant G. K. Warren, who mapped the peak during a military expedition to the Black Hills in 1857. Valentine McGillycuddy also climbed the peak in the nineteenth century, completing the ascent in 1875 at the age of twenty-six. McGillycuddy mapped the peak and also photographed it. Later he served as an agent on the Pine Ridge Reservation and as the first president of the South Dakota School of Mines. When he died in 1940, his remains were cremated and placed at the base of a fire tower that had been constructed on Harney Peak. A bronze plaque is cemented in the base of the stairway to the tower containing an inscription that reads in part WASICU WAKAN. In Lakota the words mean "holy white man."

The Civilian Conservation Corps (CCC) constructed the stone fire tower in 1938 and 1939. The CCC also constructed stone steps leading to the tower, steps that hikers still ascend today. The tower was used for detecting fires until 1967, when more modern techniques of spotting fires took over. Today the tower stands in mute testimony to the lonely life spotters led on the peak. In 1982 the structure was added to the National Register of Historic Places.

Because of its historical, geological, and spiritual significance, this lofty, craggy granite peak is home to many trails. All are worth following, for each route threads through different terrain. What's more, no two days spent wandering along the peak's crest ever offer the same experience. Each season is different too, and in years of light snowfall the trails are accessible year-round.

Harney Peak Fire Lookout, built by the CCC between 1938 and 1939, provides a commanding view of four states. ▶

Two trailheads in the northwest corner of Custer State Park lead to Harney Peak: the **Sylvan Lake Trailhead** and the **Little Devils Tower Trailhead.** Within the Black Elk Wilderness, on the northwest fringe of Custer State Park, almost 17 miles of hiking trails lead to Harney Peak from almost any direction.

NOTE: Visitors need a park entrance permit when hiking any trails within Custer State Park. The Harney Range complex is managed by the Forest Service, and all users must complete and possess a free wilderness-use registration form when hiking in the Black Elk Wilderness area. Bikes are *not* allowed on most trails in this area.

25 Sylvan Lake to Harney Peak Trail

A moderately difficult, much-used trail to spiritual Harney Peak with spectacular and varied scenery along the way. It's the highest peak east of the main chain of the Rocky Mountains.

Start: From the Sylvan Lake day-use area, following the "#9" blazes on trees.

Distance: 6.8 miles out and back.

Approximate hiking time: 4 to 6 hours.

Difficulty: Moderately difficult, due to a steep final mile to the peak.

Seasons: Best spring through fall.

Other trail users: Horses.

Land status: Custer State Park, Black Hills National Forest.

Fees and permits: Hikers will need a park entrance permit when in Custer State Park. A free Wilderness Use Registration form (available along the trails) is required for the Black Elk Wilderness Area.

Traffic: Very heavy at times, especially during summer. This is the main route to Harney Peak and averages 300 people a day.

Maps: Custer State Park Trail Guide, free and available at entrance stations and visitor centers; National Geographic/Trails Illustrated Topo Map No. 238; Black Hills National Forest Map; USGS Custer quad.

Trail contacts: Custer State Park, HC 83, Box 70, Custer, SD 57730 (605-255-4515), or Black Hills National Forest Supervisor's Office and Visitor Center, RR 2, Box 200, Custer, SD 57730 (605-673-2251); www.theblack hills.com.

Finding the trailhead: Take South Dakota Highway 89 north from Custer for 6 miles to the Sylvan Lake entrance station. Follow signs to Sylvan Lake.

Or from Peter Norbeck Visitor Center in Custer State Park, take U.S. Highway 16A west to South Dakota Highway 87 north (the Needles Highway) to Sylvan Lake, a distance of 19 miles. Access the trail from the Sylvan Lake Day-Use area. Follow blazes of "#9" on trees. The blazes are not always distinct.

The Hike

The trail provides an easy to moderate ascent for the first mile, then descends gently to the Midway area by Lost Cabin Creek, entering the Black Elk Wilderness Area. This area has no facilities. Water from the creek should not be consumed unless purified. During the initial ascent, hikers encounter a rocky outcrop with outstanding views of Harney Peak and its surroundings.

After the Midway area, the trail ascends once more, reaching a ridge that is fairly flat. About 0.25 mile later the Norbeck Trail #3 joins the trail from the right (south). Continue north following the "#9" blazes on trees. The final ascent of about 1 mile is steep with several switchbacks. It is flanked by stands of ponderosa pine and granite formations; in spring and summer wildflowers abound. Close to the summit, the trail is sprinkled with mica.

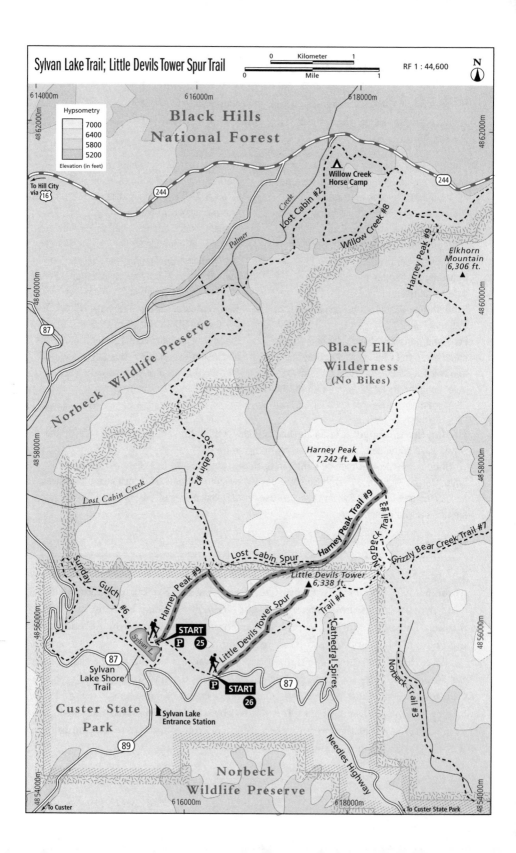

Sylvan Lake Trail; Little Devils Tower Spur Trail

0 — Kilometer — 1
0 — Mile — 1

RF 1 : 44,600

N

Black Hills National Forest

Hypsometry
7000
6400
5800
5200
Elevation (in feet)

To Hill City via (16)

(244)

Palmer Creek

Lost Cabin #2

Willow Creek Horse Camp

Willow Creek #8

(244)

Harney Peak #9

Elkhorn Mountain 6,306 ft. ▲

(87)

Norbeck Wildlife Preserve

Black Elk Wilderness (No Bikes)

Lost Cabin #2

Lost Cabin Creek

Harney Peak 7,242 ft. ▲

Harney Peak Trail #9

Norbeck Trail #3

Grizzly Bear Creek Trail #7

Sunday Gulch #6

Lost Cabin Spur

Harney Peak #9

Little Devils Tower 6,338 ft. ▲

Trail #4

START P 25

Little Devils Tower Spur

Sylvan L.

Sylvan Lake Shore Trail

(87)

P START 26

(87)

Cathedral Spires

Norbeck Trail #3

Custer State Park

Sylvan Lake Entrance Station ▲

(89)

Needles Highway

Norbeck Wildlife Preserve

To Custer

To Custer State Park

Stone and mortar steps facilitate the final climb through the rocks. Group consensus proclaims the grunt to the top, at 7,242 feet, is worth the effort. The views of four different states rolling off and eventually merging with the horizon are inspiring. To the north, in the not-so-great distance, looms the backside of Mount Rushmore, while to the south, at a distance of about 1 mile, rugged Little Devils Tower juts to a height of 6,338 feet.

In the immediate vicinity rock formations lace the area; the fire tower (no longer in use) straddles the most lofty of these. On clear days the life of a fire lookout ranger could be grand, but it's easy to imagine times when winds buffeted the tower and lightning threaded the drab sky or stabbed night's inky cloak, striking the tower and engulfing it with Saint Elmo's fire.

Because of Harney Peak's grandeur, be prepared for crowds. Thunderstorms, particularly in July and August, are frequent and produce hail and lightning. At times the sun blazes, so carry plenty of water, especially in summer.

Miles and Directions

0.0 Start at the Sylvan Lake day-use area. Access Harney Peak Trail #9, which is blazed on trees. You'll head northwest.

0.75 The Lost Cabin Trail enters from the north (left). Stay on #9 to your right (east).

1.4 Enter the Black Elk Wilderness; portal registration required.

2.6 There's an intersection with Norbeck Trail #3 from the south (right). Stay straight (north) on #9.

3.4 Arrive at Harney Peak.

6.8 Return to Sylvan Lake by the same route.

26 Little Devils Tower Spur Trail

A fairly steep hike up a spur trail, winding through pine forest and ending atop Little Devils Tower among incredible rock formations and views.

See map on page 84
Start: From the Little Devils Tower parking lot on South Dakota Highway 87 (Needles Highway).
Distance: 3 miles out and back.
Approximate hiking time: 2 to 3 hours.
Difficulty: Moderately strenuous.
Seasons: Best from spring through fall.

Other trail users: Hikers only, moderate use.
Land status: Custer State Park.
Fees and permits: Park entry permit required.
Maps: National Geographic/Trails Illustrated Topo Map No. 238; free Custer State Park Trail Guide; Black Hills National Forest Map.
Trail contact: Custer State Park, HC 83, Box 70, Custer, SD 57730; (605) 255-4515.

Finding the trailhead: The trailhead is located in Little Devils Tower parking lot, which is 1 mile east of Sylvan Lake on SD 87 (Needles Highway). From Peter Norbeck Visitor Center in Custer State Park, take U.S. Highway 16A west to SD 87 north to Little Devils Tower parking lot on the right, a total distance of about 18 miles. From the east side of the parking lot, follow the trail with "#4" blazed on trees.

The Hike

Follow Trail #4/Little Devils Tower Trail east for about 0.75 mile, crossing two small streams and walking through stands of quaking aspen and Black Hills spruce. In the right season, wildflowers such as Rocky Mountain wild iris abound. At the first trail junction, hikers have a choice: The trail to the right stays on Trail #4 and leads ultimately to Harney Peak. By taking the spur trail to the left, one accesses Little Devils Tower.

The spur trail begins almost immediately with a fairly steep ascent through ponderosa pine, low-growing juniper, and rocks that look like pancakes turned on edge and stuck in the ground. The trail then makes a sharp left turn through what appears to be a cave. But this one has no roof; the walls almost touch at the top, but not quite. The summit is reached after a steep hike of approximately forty minutes. Follow the orange blazes on and through the lichen-covered rocks and ascend to the top of Little Devils Tower at an elevation of 6,338 feet. Harney Peak is directly across the narrow valley to the north and presents a wonderful display of the formations known as the Cathedral Spires to the southeast. To the northeast is the backside of Mount Rushmore, and to the south hikers can view the rolling Black Hills. The panoramic view into the Black Hills central area is well worth the strenuous hike. In summer the trail is flanked by wildflowers such as buttercups and shooting stars.

Walking the Little Devils Tower Spur Trail isn't easy. ▶

After a well-earned rest, you must now hike back down 1.5 miles to the Little Devils Tower trailhead, where you can continue on to Harney Peak via Sylvan Lake Trail and Harney Peak Loop, or save that hike for another day. Remember that hiking off-trail in an unmarked area is not recommended or encouraged.

NOTE: From the west end of Little Devils Tower parking lot, you may take a short, marked trail west that leads to Sylvan Lake.

Miles and Directions

0.0 Start at Little Devils Tower Trailhead (#4).

0.75 Take the spur trail to northeast (left).

1.5 Arrive at Little Devils Tower.

3.0 Retrace your steps to the trailhead.

27 Little Devils Tower Trailhead to Harney Peak

A short, pleasant walk through woods with the option of linking up with several trails to Harney Peak.

Start: At the Little Devils Tower Trailhead, located 1 mile east of Sylvan Lake.
Distance: 6.2 miles out and back.
Approximate hiking time: 4 to 6 hours.
Difficulty: Moderate to strenuous.
Seasons: Best from spring through fall.
Other trail users: Horses.
Land status: Custer State Park, Black Hills National Forest.
Fees and permits: A Custer State Park entrance permit and a free Wilderness Use Registration Permit.

Maps: National Geographic/Trails Illustrated Topo Map No. 238; Custer State Park Trail Guide, free at entrance stations and visitor centers; Black Hills National Forest Map.
Trail contacts: Custer State Park, HC 83, Box 70, Custer, SD 57730 (605-255-4515), or Black Hills National Forest Supervisor's Office and Visitor Center, RR 2, Box 200, Custer, SD 57730 (605-673-2251); www.theblack hills.com.

Finding the trailhead: The trail leaves from the east end of the Little Devils Tower parking lot, which is located 1 mile east of Sylvan Lake on South Dakota Highway 87 (Needles Highway).

The Hike

This short trail, blazed with "#4," begins as an easy, flat ramble through the woods, and continues that way for about 0.75 mile to a trail junction. This could be a turn-around point for a short walk. If you wish to continue hiking, stay to the right at the junction; the left trail is the spur to Little Devils Tower.

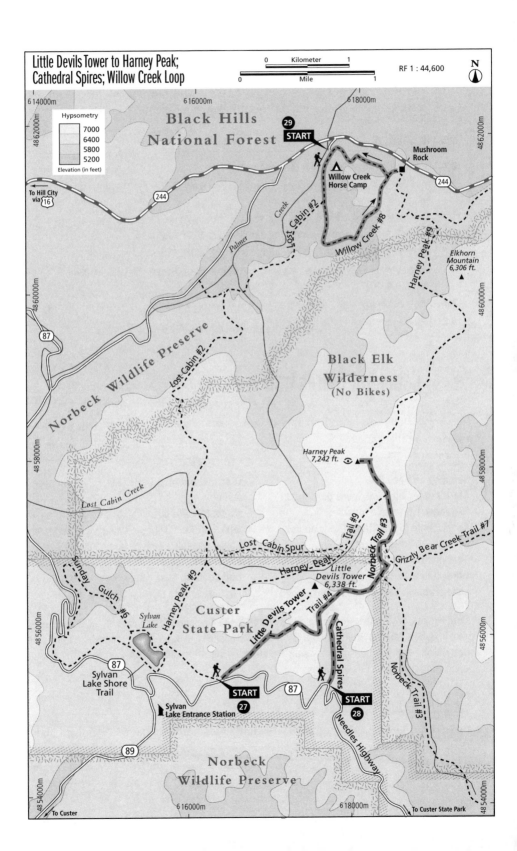

Little Devils Tower to Harney Peak;
Cathedral Spires; Willow Creek Loop

Kilometer

RF 1 : 44,600

N

Mile

Hypsometry
7000
6400
5800
5200
Elevation (in feet)

Black Hills
National Forest

29 START

Mushroom
Rock

Willow Creek
Horse Camp

244

To Hill City
via 16

244

Palmer

Creek

Lost Cabin #2

Willow Creek #8

Harney Peak #9

Elkhorn
Mountain
6,306 ft.

87

Norbeck Wildlife Preserve

Lost Cabin #2

Black Elk
Wilderness
(No Bikes)

Harney Peak
7,242 ft.

Lost Cabin Creek

Lost Cabin Spur

Harney Peak Trail #9

Norbeck Trail #3

Grizzly Bear Creek Trail #7

Sunday Gulch #6

Harney Peak #9

Sylvan
Lake

Custer
State Park

Little
Devils Tower
6,338 ft.

Trail #4

Little Devils Tower

Cathedral Spires

Norbeck Trail #3

87

Sylvan
Lake Shore
Trail

START 27

87

START 28

Sylvan Lake Entrance Station

Needles Highway

89

Norbeck
Wildlife Preserve

To Custer

616000m

618000m

To Custer State Park

To go on to Harney Peak, take the right-hand route, blazed #4. After a twenty-to thirty-minute ascent through stands of ponderosa, you will connect with the Norbeck Trail #3. Take #3 left (north) for a little over 1 mile and connect with the Harney Peak Trail #9, going straight (north), then continue on to Harney Peak.

Miles and Directions

0.0 Start at the Little Devils Tower Trailhead (#4).

0.75 The junction with Little Devils Tower Spur Trail is on the left. Stay right (northeast) on Trail #4.

1.75 This is the junction with Norbeck Trail #3. Turn left (north) on #3. Fill out free Wilderness Use Registration, as you are entering the Black Elk Wilderness area.

2.0 Grizzly Bear Creek Trail #7 comes in from the right (east). Stay straight (north) on #3.

2.5 Sylvan Lake/Harney Peak Trail #9 comes in from the left. Access #9, going straight ahead (north).

3.1 Arrive at Harney Peak.

6.2 Retrace your steps to the trailhead.

28 Cathedral Spires Trail

This moderately strenuous spur trail is a great natural-history trek, offering wonderful views of the spires.

See map on page 89
Start: At the Cathedral Spires parking lot.
Distance: 1.5 miles out and back.
Approximate hiking time: 1 to 2 hours.
Difficulty: Moderate to strenuous.
Seasons: Best from spring through fall.
Other trail users: Hikers only.
Land status: Custer State Park.

Fees and permits: Custer State Park entrance permit.
Maps: National Geographic/Trails Illustrated Topo Map No. 238; free Custer State Park Trail Guide available at entrance stations and visitor centers.
Trail contact: Custer State Park, HC 83, Box 70, Custer, SD 57730; (605) 255-4515.

Finding the trailhead: The trail is accessed from the Cathedral Spires parking lot, 2.5 miles east of Sylvan Lake on South Dakota Highway 87 (Needles Highway). You can access it from Custer State Park's Peter Norbeck Visitor Center by taking U.S. Highway 16A west to SD 87 and going north for a total of 16.5 miles.

The Hike

In 1977 Congress proclaimed the Cathedral Spires Trail a registered National Landmark. Limber pine—a five-needled pine tree—grows some distance in from the trail. To find this same species elsewhere, one must travel hundreds of miles north or go west to the Big Horn Mountains. Core samplings indicate that the limber pines here are hundreds of years old. The question is, how did they ever establish themselves along this remote trail deep within the Black Hills of South Dakota? Glaciologists say that some ten thousand years ago, massive ice fields isolated these stands of *Pinus flexilus*. Other scientists theorize that the trees' seeds were brought into the area by bird droppings. Whatever happened, limber pine now grows along this trail as an isolated community that remains peculiar to the Black Hills.

Hikers might ponder the mystery of the pines as well as other Black Hills' phenomena as they hike the beautiful and inspiring Cathedral Spires Trail. The path winds and climbs among fantastic formations that also contributed to the trail's national designation. In places these spires descend to the trail's very edges.

The Cathedral Spires Trail is a somewhat strenuous hike that begins at the east end of the parking area. At first the trail is flat, but after crossing a creek (the depth of which will depend on the amount of rainfall that year), it quickly begins its ascent and, with few exceptions, never stops. Game trails lace the area, and because they can at times be confused with the main trail, pay close attention to the progression of marked trees. If you lose sight of them, simply stay between the confines of the narrow valley walls until you link once again with the main trail.

Once the trail climbs through the narrow U of rock bluffs, it widens and becomes much more distinct. On top of the first saddle, projecting from about 30 feet overhead, looms what many have imagined is the figure of a robed man sculpted in rock by nature's forces. The trail dead-ends here, on the north side of the spires. Now you must backtrack downhill.

29 Willow Creek Loop

An easy loop trail that provides periodic vistas of Harney Peak.

See map on page 89
Start: From the Willow Creek Horse Camp on South Dakota Highway 244.
Distance: 1.5-mile loop.
Approximate hiking time: 1½ to 2 hours.
Difficulty: Easy.
Seasons: Best spring through fall.
Other trail users: Heavy horse use.
Land status: Black Hills National Forest.

Fees and permits: N/A
Maps: National Geographic/Trails Illustrated Topo Map No. 238; Black Hills National Forest Map; USGS Hill City and Custer quads.
Trail contact: Black Hills National Forest Supervisor's Office and Visitor Center, RR 2, Box 200, Custer, SD 57730; (605) 673-2251; www.theblackhills.com.

Finding the trailhead: The trailhead is located at Willow Creek Horse Camp on SD 244, about 4 miles east of the turnoff onto SD 244 from U.S. Highways 16/385. From the east, Willow Creek Horse Camp is about 4 miles west of the Mount Rushmore Memorial on SD 244 (opposite Palmer Creek KOA).

Walk among tall trees and giant boulders on Willow Creek–Sylvan Lake #9 Trail.

The Hike

Willow Creek Loop Trail provides vistas of Harney Peak, a bird's-eye view of the spires of Elkhorn Mountain, and a stroll through stands of some of the Black Hills' largest ponderosa pines. Starting from Willow Creek Horse Camp, one can either proceed southwest on Trails #2 and #8 or northeast on Trail #9. Along the way, short spur trails lead from the main trail. One short spur takes hikers to a small dam on Willow Creek. Depending on the season and the year, Willow Creek can be a full flow or a quiet seep.

About 1 mile (assuming you are proceeding in a counterclockwise direction) from the trailhead, a 600-foot-long spur trail ascends to Mushroom Rock. Here, hikers are offered views of Harney Peak and the spires of Elkhorn Mountain. Mushroom Rock is a large rock outcropping that has been sculpted by weathering into a shape that could only be named as it is.

Because the trail access is directly across the highway from a KOA campground, this loop hike provides exceptional access for KOA campers and for those camped at the Willow Creek Campground.

Miles and Directions

0.0 Start at the Willow Creek Horse Camp trailhead.

1.0 Hiking counterclockwise, you encounter a spur trail to Mushroom Rock.

1.5 Complete the loop.

30 Harney Peak Loop

A series of trails providing an outing through wilderness and some exceptional wildlife habitat. Hikers eventually reach Harney Peak.

Start: From Iron Creek Horse Camp trailhead.
Distance: 10.5-mile lollipop.
Approximate hiking time: All day, or add an overnight.
Difficulty: Strenuous, particularly if the entire 10.5 miles are hiked in a single day.
Seasons: From spring through fall.
Other trail users: Horses.
Land status: Custer State Park, Black Hills National Forest.
Fees and permits: Hikers will need a park entrance permit when in Custer State Park. A free Wilderness Use Registration form (avail-able along the trails) is required for the Black Elk Wilderness Area.
Maps: National Geographic/Trails Illustrated Topo Map No. 238; Forest Service handout of Harney Peak area; Black Hills National Forest Map; USGS Mount Rushmore, Iron Mountain, and Custer quads.
Trail contacts: Custer State Park, HC 83, Box 70, Custer, SD 57730 (605-255-4515), or Black Hills National Forest Supervisor's Office and Visitor Center, RR 2, Box 200, Custer, SD 57730 (605-673-2251); www.theblack hills.com.

Finding the trailhead: Although the drive to reach the trailhead begins in Custer State Park, the trailhead is just over the boundary in Black Hills National Forest. The trek begins at Iron Creek Horse Camp. To reach the trailhead, take U.S. Highway 16A west from the park's Peter Norbeck Visitor Center to South Dakota Highway 87 (Needles Highway) and go north for a total of about 7 miles. A sign on the right to Iron Creek Horse Camp indicates your turn. Follow the dirt road about 0.5 mile, then take the first road to the left and park at the road's end.

The Hike

For those interested in a challenging hike, this combination of four different trails provides just that. Because the distance is lengthy, some consideration should be given to camping in the Black Elk Wilderness, named for the famous Oglala medicine man who was present as a young teenager at the Battle of the Little Bighorn. Water is plentiful, though it must be purified, and primitive wilderness campsites are abundant. Before pitching your tent, however, check that you are not camped in a patch of poison ivy. Practice zero-impact ethics.

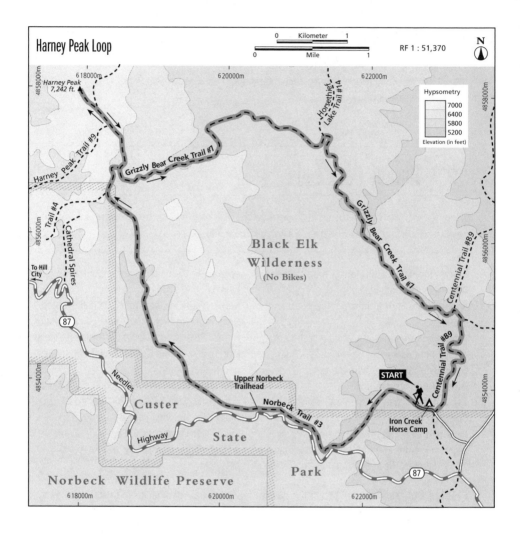

The trail, heading west-southwest, begins as a dirt road at the trailhead at the end of the road on the northwest edge of Iron Creek Horse Camp, but 0.1 mile later it becomes a more traditional trail and what will eventually be the return route from Harney Peak. Shortly thereafter the trail crosses what is often an insignificant Iron Creek, as far as stream crossings go. At this point the trail sign says NORBECK TRAIL #3.

At the beginning of the hike, much of the forest consists of bur oak, ponderosa pine, quaking aspen, and some paper birch. The bottom portion of the trail is wide, but as it begins to ascend, the trail narrows and soon passes over several small saddles. About 2 miles out from the trailhead, the trail approaches and parallels the Needles Highway for about 1 mile. It then passes another possible access site, the Upper Norbeck Trailhead, where there is a registration panel for the Black Elk Wilderness.

Grizzly Bear Creek Trail takes you through the Harney Ranger District.

From here the trail begins to climb abruptly to the north. Soon hikers are rewarded with close-up views of jumbled rock formations. Equally impressive are the many trees that have managed to establish footholds among these seemingly impenetrable boulders. This part of the trail passes through the west side of the Black Elk Wilderness Area.

About 3.5 miles from the Iron Creek trailhead, hikers link with the Sylvan Lake/Harney Peak Trail #9, which enters from the west and continues to Harney Peak. After the 1.5-mile climb to Harney Peak and back on Trail #9, pick up the Grizzly Bear Creek Trail #7 to your left, and begin what is essentially a continuous descent. Backpackers should note that they are in the Black Elk Wilderness and that camping options are numerous, but camping is not allowed within 0.25 mile of Harney Peak or within 150 feet of a trail. Practice zero-impact camping rules so that others who follow will have an equally good wilderness experience.

Because you are in a wilderness, bridges across streams are lacking. Consequently the numerous stream crossings may result in wet feet, ankles, and sometimes even thighs unless one finds a stable log or two. Vegetation on the descent is similar to

More than 70 miles of trails lead to Harney Peak, the highest peak east of the Rockies.

what was encountered during the ascent, except for the last 3 miles. Here you'll see evidence of beaver activity, which provides you with what certainly is one of the best examples in the Black Hills of the industriousness of this enterprising mammal. The dams constructed by these creatures vary in length from 75 yards to but a few feet. Beavers have modified the area's entire ecology, creating habitat upon which many other species are dependent. White-tailed deer feed on the grasses, and the impoundments created by the dams attract ducks of various species. The rushes and cattails provide prime habitat for red-winged blackbirds. About 3 miles from trail's end, you can count on wet boots, or include a pair of wading tennis shoes in your pack.

In another 1.5 miles, the trail converges with the Centennial Trail from the north. Continue south at this junction on Grizzly Bear Creek Trail for several hundred yards until reaching the signpost for CENTENNIAL TRAIL #89, heading due south. Continue on this trail, which winds through rocks and woods for 1.5 miles before ending at the Iron Creek trailhead, just east of where the hike began.

Miles and Directions

0.0 Start at the Iron Creek Horse Camp trailhead, Norbeck Trail #3.

2.0 Reach the Upper Iron Creek trailhead (Norbeck Trail #3).

3.0 Sylvan Lake–Harney Trail #9 is encountered from the west. Take #9 north.

4.5 Reach Harney Peak. Begin return of loop by taking Trail #9 to the right (south) as you leave Harney Peak.

5.0 Trail #9 (Sylvan Lake) bears to the right. Stay straight on what will now be Norbeck Trail #3.

5.5 Grizzly Bear Creek Trail #7 comes in from your left and heads east. Take this trail (#7).

7.5 Horsethief Lake Trail joins from the north. Stay heading south on #7.

9.3 Centennial Trail #89 comes in from the north. Stay on #7.

9.5 Centennial Trail #89 joins from the south. Take this trail.

10.5 Return to Iron Creek Horse Camp.

31 Lost Cabin–Harney Peak Loop

A vigorous loop hike through a variety of lofty terrain so beautiful that one of the trails (Lost Cabin) has been designated a National Recreational Trail.

Start: From Willow Creek Horse Camp trailhead.

Distance: 8.6-mile loop.

Approximate hiking time: Count on nearly a full day.

Difficulty: Strenuous.

Seasons: Best from spring through fall.

Other trail users: Horses.

Land status: Black Hills National Forest (Norbeck Wildlife Preserve and Black Elk Wilderness).

Fees and permits: A free Wilderness Use Registration needed; forms are found at registration boxes along the way.

Maps: National Geographic/Trails Illustrated Topo Map No. 238; free Forest Service trail handout of Harney Peak area; Black Hills National Forest Map.

Trail contact: Black Hills National Forest Supervisor's Office and Visitor Center, RR 2, Box 200, Custer, SD 57730; (605) 673-2251; www.theblackhills.com.

Finding the trailhead: The Lost Cabin Trail trailhead is located at Willow Creek Horse Camp on South Dakota Highway 244 across from the Palmer Creek KOA, which is approximately 3 miles east off U.S. Highways 16/385 out of Custer or 4 miles west of Mount Rushmore.

The Hike

Part of the Harney Trail system, this hike may be one of the most picturesque in the interior. It is somewhat less strenuous if followed in the direction suggested here, but those desiring a more strenuous hike can reverse the loop. Plan to spend most of a day on this hike; you will want to stop often to absorb the views.

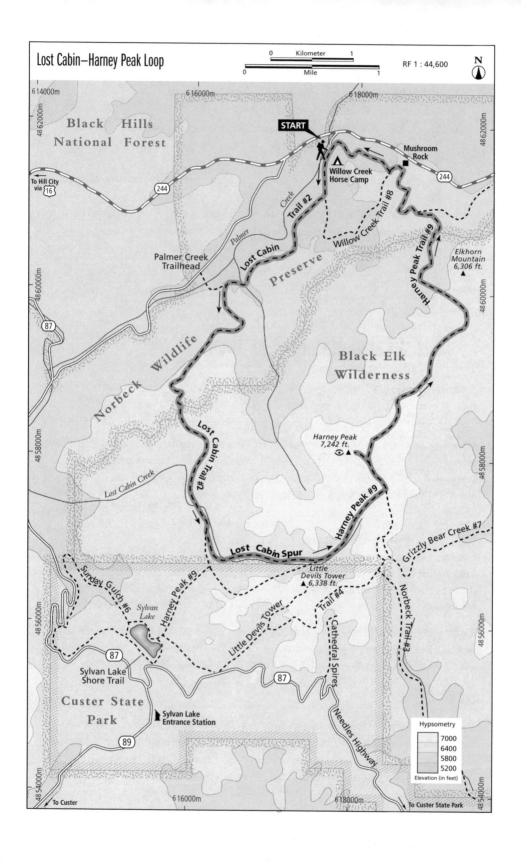

A trail of such immense appeal it has been designated as one of the two National Recreation Trails in the Black Hills National Forest, the Lost Cabin Trail #2 is quickly accessed by departing from Willow Creek Horse Camp and following the sign for Trail #2. The Lost Cabin Trail immediately ascends through numerous rock outcroppings and stands of ponderosa pine and birch to a saddle. At the saddle the trail begins a series of gentle ups and downs, though the general grade is up. About 0.75 mile from the trailhead, take the left trail, which crosses Nelson Creek. About 0.25 mile later you will encounter a second major junction. The trail to the west (right), ends up at the Palmer Creek trailhead; stay left.

Follow Trail #2 south (left) and ascend to a wide saddle. At one point along the 1-mile ascent, you'll see the remains of old mining cabins. In July the trailsides are sprinkled with a variety of wildflowers. Look for camas, Indian paintbrush, harebell, and yarrow. Juniper berries weigh heavy on the low-growing bushes. At the saddle a small copse of birch graces the trail edge. To the west is a rock outcropping that provides views of Sunday Gulch and Saint Elmo's Peak.

The trail levels for a short distance then climbs moderately. At this point the elevation is 6,320 feet. After entering the wilderness, the trail undulates mildly, soon crossing a small stream and entering a parklike setting. In summer bunchberry dogwood blossoms by the stream and the smell of wild mint is strong. Spire and needle formations surround the trail.

From the stream, the Lost Cabin Spur continues for another 1 to 1.25 miles where it concludes as it joins with the Harney Peak Trail #9. Or you can dip south at the first junction with Harney Peak Trail #9. Hike east (left) on Trail #9, climbing another 0.75 mile until you reach the Harney Peak spur trail on the left. Ascend the short, steep spur trail to Harney Peak.

Descend from Harney Peak and resume hiking along the Harney Peak Trail #9 by turning left and heading north. The trail retains the designation of Willow Creek/Harney Peak #9 from this point until its terminus at Willow Creek Horse Camp. This trail is mislabeled on some older Trails Illustrated maps, but the map legend is correct. The initial descent is steep. For the next mile the trail makes no fewer than thirty switchbacks as it plummets 500 feet. The trail then levels to a saddle offering superb views of Harney Peak, the backside of Mount Rushmore, and surrounding spire formations. Here, facing east, one can clearly see the Hog Back Ridge and Red Valley, which engulf the granite formations of the Central Area of the Black Hills. In the more distant east, the Badlands suggest a great mystery as they blend with the horizon.

For the next 2 miles, the trail descends and winds through ponderosa pine, eroded pinnacles and spires, and boulder fields of Elkhorn Mountain. At an intersection 2 miles before trail's end, swing northwest (left) onto a winding, old dirt road, following trail signs for Willow Creek Trailhead, where this hike concludes.

Miles and Directions

0.0 Start at the Willow Creek Horse Camp trailhead. Head south, following signs for the Lost Cabin Trail #2.

0.75 Cross Nelson Creek.

1.0 The trail to Palmer Creek trailhead comes in from the right. Do not take this trail.

3.5 This is the junction with Harney Peak Trail #9. Take the Lost Cabin Spur to the left, but you could follow Harney Peak Trail to the southeast then curve back northeast.

4.7 The trail intersects with Norbeck Trail #3 from the right (south). Turn left here (north), staying on Harney Peak Trail #9.

5.2 Arrive at Harney Peak. Descend from Harney Peak, go left (north) on Harney Peak Trail #9 toward Willow Creek Horse Camp.

7.6 Willow Creek–Rushmore Trail #5 goes east (right). Continue left to the northwest on #9 toward Willow Creek Horse Camp.

8.6 Return to the Willow Creek Horse Camp trailhead.

32 Iron Mountain Loop

A loop hike taking hikers from mountaintop to forest floor while threading over streams, into small valleys flanked by rock formations, and through parklike settings cut by beaver dams.

Start: At the Iron Mountain Picnic Area on Iron Mountain Road.
Distance: 5.1-mile lollipop.
Approximate hiking time: 4 hours.
Difficulty: Easy to moderate.
Seasons: Best from spring through fall.
Other trail users: Horses.
Land status: Black Hills National Forest, Black Elk Wilderness Area.

Fees and permits: Free Wilderness Use Registration form required; the panel with forms is located directly west of the parking area.
Maps: National Geographic/Trails Illustrated Topo Map No. 238; Black Hills National Forest Map; USGS Hill City and Custer quads.
Trail contact: Black Hills National Forest Supervisor's Office and Visitor Center, RR 2, Box 200, Custer, SD 57730; (605) 673-2251; www.theblackhills.com.

Finding the trailhead: From the Peter Norbeck Visitor Center in Custer State Park, take U.S. Highway 16A east for 1 mile. Take the left fork at the sign for Iron Mountain Road and follow that for 2 miles. Take a left onto Iron Mountain Road (US 16A) toward Mount Rushmore for 12.9 miles to the trailhead sign on the left. You are in the Peter Norbeck Wildlife Preserve, south of Mount Rushmore. The trail begins at the west end of the parking area for the Iron Mountain Picnic Area. Restroom facilities, water, and picnic tables are available here.

The Iron Mountain Trail courses through an area of mountain goat country as it approaches a saddle between rugged rock formations.

The Hike

The Iron Mountain Trail is a day trip that provides hikers with glimpses of the many facets of the Black Hills. The trail is also open in most parts to horseback riders. This trail is entirely in the wilderness, and bikes are not allowed in the wilderness areas; signs are posted to that effect. From the parking lot, follow the asphalt path past the toilets to access the trailhead.

The trail begins as a wide dirt trail blazed "#89B." It heads west and, at 0.5 mile, joins the Iron Mountain Trail #16, which goes south (left) and which you follow. The trail is well marked with "#16" blazed on trees. In this area of fascinating rock formations, look for a unique one shaped exactly like a turtle. Here, the trail appears to be an old four-wheel-drive road.

After approximately 1.2 miles the trail meets an improved gravel road (Forest Road 345). Go west-southwest (right) on the road. Follow the dirt road for about 1 mile, where five bridges cross Iron Creek as it meanders through the mountains. Take the next trail to the northwest (right), where the trail sign indicates Grizzly

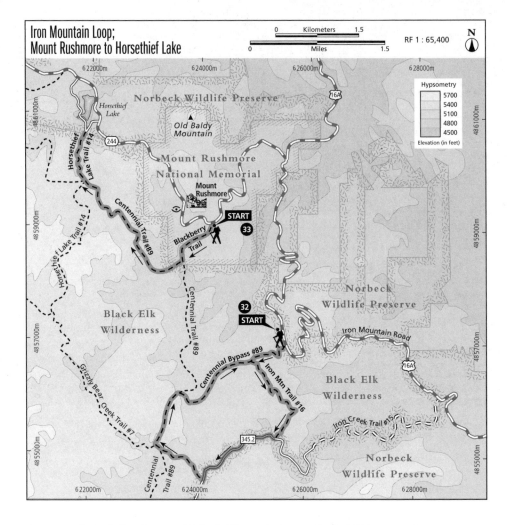

Bear Creek Trail #7, Centennial Trail #89, and Harney Peak. Hiking now in a west-erly, slightly northwesterly direction, you'll see inspiring rock formations. In the fall the yellow- and rust-colored leaves intermingle with the dark green of the pon-derosa pine, lending even more drama to the igneous rock. Small mammals hide here, and you might catch (as we did) glimpses of an elusive mink.

After another 0.5 mile the trail takes a hard right (the trail sign indicates Cen-tennial Trail #89, Mount Rushmore, Centennial Bypass 89B) and heads north for 0.75 mile, where you'll encounter yet another junction. Follow the trail signs for 1.2 miles to the northeast (right) on #89B, thus completing the loop. This is an easy to moderate trek of two to four hours, presenting great vistas.

Another optional hike of about 4.2 miles in this same area begins in the same manner as described above. Upon reaching FR 345, however, go southeast (left) on the road for about 0.75 mile to the Iron Creek Trail #15. Mountain biking is allowed

Iron Creek Trail crosses the Black Elk Wilderness, which was named for the revered Native American holy man Ben Black Elk.

on this trail only. The northern edge of the trail begins the wilderness area and is well marked. This 2-mile trail is an easy trek going due east. It follows old roads through meadows and ponderosa pine until it terminates at Lakota Lake Trailhead, adjacent to the Iron Mountain Highway. Of course, doing this one-way hike requires a shuttle between Lakota Lake and the Iron Mountain Picnic Area.

Miles and Directions

- **0.0** Start at the Iron Mountain Picnic Area trailhead. Take the asphalt path past the toilets to access the trail, blazed "89B."
- **0.5** Go south (left) at the junction with Iron Mountain Trail #16.
- **1.7** Head southwest (right) on FR 345.
- **2.7** Take Grizzly Bear Creek Trail #7 west (right).
- **3.2** Go north (right) at the junction with Centennial Trail #89.
- **3.9** At the junction take Centennial Bypass (89B) to the east.
- **5.1** Return to the Iron Mountain Picnic Area trailhead.

33 Mount Rushmore to Horsethief Lake

An extremely scenic out-and-back hike departing from Mount Rushmore and terminating at Horsethief Lake, with access to other trails, some leading to Harney Peak.

See map on page 102
Start: Across South Dakota Highway 244 from the southern end of the Mount Rushmore parking lot. There is a small trailhead panel here with map.
Distance: 6 miles out and back.
Approximate hiking time: 2 to 3 hours.
Difficulty: Easy to moderate.
Seasons: Best from spring through fall.
Other trail users: Heavy horse use on Blackberry Trail.

Land status: Black Hills National Forest.
Fees and permits: N/A
Maps: National Geographic/Trails Illustrated Topo Map No. 238; Black Hills National Forest Map; free Forest Service Harney Peak trails handout; USGS Mount Rushmore quad.
Trail contact: Black Hills National Forest Supervisor's Office and Visitor Center, RR 2, Box 200, Custer, SD 57730; (605) 673-2251; www.theblackhills.com.

Finding the trailhead: The trailhead is located at the southern end of the Mount Rushmore parking lot. Cross SD 244 on the curve with a highway railing. Climb over the railing and the well-used dirt trail is easily discernible. Here you'll find a small trailhead panel with a map. Overnight parking is not allowed in the memorial.

The Hike

The trail markers, encountered almost immediately after winding through rocks and pine, read "#8." This path (Blackberry Trail) is the only trail leading away from Mount Rushmore, and you're only on it for about 0.5 mile, where you'll soon encounter a T intersection with Centennial Trail #89. Head west/northwest (to the right).

For 2 miles the trail winds up and down through a ponderosa-pine forest until another trail junction is encountered. Here you'll have several options. If continuing to Horsethief Lake, go due north (right) at this junction on Horsethief Lake Trail #14 for about 0.75 mile into Horsethief Lake. This is a peaceful and very picturesque hike, particularly when birch and aspen leaves are turning in autumn. The trail parallels and crosses a stream with several small, beautiful waterfalls. Granite rock formations rise steeply on each side, giving the sensation of entering an area known by no one else. If this is your final destination, backtrack from here.

The other options at the trail junction mentioned above are as follows: Follow Horsethief Lake Trail #14 south (left) for 2 miles to the junction with Grizzly Bear Creek Trail #7. An easy to moderate walk, this route offers hikers magnificent views of the entire Harney Peak area as it ambles through lofty peaks and spires. The Horsethief Lake Trail ends here at Grizzly Bear Creek Trail #7.

Several trails in the Harney Range lead to Mount Rushmore. Others provide periodic views of the faces carved by Gutzon Borglum.

To make a loop from this point back to Mount Rushmore, take Grizzly Bear Creek Trail #7 southeast (left) for 1.5 to 2 miles. This is a hike of moderate descent that is partly a trail and partly an old four-wheel-drive road passing through meadows and past beaver ponds flanked by rock wall formations. The trail continues uninterrupted until Centennial Trail #89 joins from the north. Take this trail north for slightly more than 3 miles, following signs for Mount Rushmore. The ascent is moderate as the trail passes through pine forests and unique rocks, offering views of the surrounding peaks. The Blackberry Trail enters from the northeast (right); take that for 0.5 mile to SD 244 and the parking lot at Mount Rushmore.

To access Harney Peak from the point where the Horsethief Lake Trail ends, backtrack to the junction with Grizzly Bear Creek Trail #7 and go west/northwest (right). This 2.25-mile hike is strenuous as it ascends 1,000 feet in the final 1.5 miles. A lightly used trail, the route brings hikers to the solitude and peace of the Black Elk Wilderness. As the Grizzly Bear Creek Trail ends, hikers should take the Harney

Peak Trail #9 north (right) to the summit of Harney Peak, about 1 mile farther. This is a strenuous hike and adds miles and hours to your day, so give good thought and planning to this suggestion.

Miles and Directions

0.0 Start at the Blackberry trailhead across SD 244 from the Mount Rushmore parking lot.

0.5 Encounter a T intersection with Centennial Trail #89. Go west-northwest (right).

2.25 Stay north (right) at junction with Horsethief Lake Trail #14 and Willow Creek-Rushmore Trail.

3.0 Arrive at Horsethief Lake.

6.0 Backtrack your route to return to the parking lot at Mount Rushmore.

Deerfield

n 1874, two years before the infamous battle along Montana's Little Bighorn River, Lt. Col. George A. Custer led his U.S. Army troops into the Black Hills. Custer was looking for a site that might be appropriate for constructing a fort. Accordingly, a cartographer traveled with the Seventh Cavalry and helped map much of the Black Hills. With this information, settlers soon followed, since the Custer Expedition also helped secure the area against Indians determined to defend the integrity of the Paha Sapa. These were their spiritual grounds, a place where many traveled in search of vision quests. The discovery of gold changed all that. Though the Black Hills were promised by treaty to the Sioux, the lure of gold was too great, and the promises were broken. The fate of the Sioux in the Black Hills was sealed.

During this 1874 expedition, Custer and his men camped on Castle Creek at what eventually became known as Deerfield (first known as Mountain City). Deerfield was the site of a brief gold rush, and a small town evolved there and remained until 1940, at which time developers moved the store, school, post office, and other buildings to make way for the impoundment resulting from construction of Deerfield Dam.

Other mining towns also evolved, and several still linger along the route traversed by the Deerfield Trail. Canyon City, just below the mouth of Slate Creek, took root between the 1880s and 1890s, when men worked placer mines here. Silver City, near trail's end, was once home to 300 people, many of whom dug for gold, silver, antimony, and mercury. Today only a few residents remain.

The Silver City Trailhead is located at the end of town on Rapid Creek, a great trout-fishing stream. The Deerfield Trail, completed in 1992, and its associated Lake Loop Trail expose a slice of history unique to the Black Hills.

The Deerfield Trail also approaches three other towns that at one time hummed with activity and the thud and pound of dredge, ax, and shovel. Two of these are Castleton and Mystic. Though the town site of Castleton has faded with time, Mystic retains a number of its structures. As a result of its history, much of the small village has been placed on the National Register of Historic Places. Mystic was first named Sitting Bull by miners in 1876. As the town developed and the mining activity flourished, railroad tracks were laid. These carried trains as recently as 1983. One of the town's most long-lived operations was a sawmill, which provided jobs for other residents and which operated until 1952. Today the George S. Mickelson Trail (hike

Deerfield Overview

Kilometers
RF 1 : 118,500

N

56) links with the Deerfield Trail near the Mystic Trailhead and directs trail users to Mystic, less than a mile away. The Deerfield Trail and the George S. Mickelson Trail are sometimes one and the same.

Hikers and bikers often follow the old Grand Island & Wyoming Central Railroad (later the Burlington Northern) rail lines. Those who hike to Castleton and Mystic are traveling along this old rail line. As well as slicing through much of the nation's mining and railroad history and South Dakota's in particular, the Deerfield Trail provides access to some of the state's best fishing. Deerfield Lake offers anglers the opportunity to catch rainbow trout. The more eastern portions of the trail provide access to brown-trout fisheries. One eastern portion of the trail is a designated walk-in fishery and prohibits all motorized vehicle use.

The Deerfield Trail passes through some of the most spectacular country in the Black Hills, an area abundant with wildlife. Look to the meadows for white-tailed deer, to the streams for beaver, and the woods for turkey.

One Forest Service ranger who has hiked the Deerfield Trail on a number of occasions suggests making it a three-day trek, camping out for two nights. One suggested campsite is about 1 mile west of the Mystic Trailhead; another is along Rapid Creek, about 2 miles west of the Silver City Trailhead. Because the elevation loss is almost 2,000 feet as one travels west to east, we recommend that you proceed in that direction.

Hill City, South Dakota, "The Heart of the Hills," may be used as the jumping-off place for roads to the various Deerfield trails. Hill City is about 28 miles southwest of Rapid City on U.S. 16. To reach Hill City from Custer, take U.S. Highways 385 and 16 north for 14 miles.

34 Deerfield Trail

Suitable for both hikers and mountain bikers, the Deerfield Trail slices through segments of the nation's history and some of the Black Hills' most pristine country.

Start: From the Custer Trailhead at Deerfield Lake on Forest Road 417.
Distance: 18 miles one-way.
Approximate hiking time: One very long day or an overnight for a 2-day trip.
Difficulty: Moderate to strenuous.
Highest elevation: Signal Knob, 6,200 feet.
Seasons: Best from late spring through fall.
Other trail users: Mountain bikers and horses.

Land status: Black Hills National Forest.
Fees and permits: N/A
Maps: Black Hills National Forest Map, available at Forest Service offices and visitor centers; USDA Forest Service Map No. 40, free from Forest Service offices and Black Hills visitor centers.
Trail contact: Black Hills National Forest Visitor Center, 23939 U.S. Highway 385, Hill City, SD 57745; (605) 343-8755.

Finding the trailheads: To reach the **Custer Trailhead** and Deerfield Lake, follow Forest Road 17 (also called Deerfield Road) northwest out of the center of Hill City for 20 miles until it intersects with FR 417. Follow FR 417 for 2 miles to Deerfield Lake and the Custer Trailhead, a total of 22 miles from Hill City. The Custer Trailhead is common to both the Deerfield Trail #40 and Deerfield Lake Loop Trail #40L.

To begin at the **Kinny Canyon Trailhead,** start in Hill City and proceed 10 miles along FR 17 until it intersects with Forest Road 188 (also called Slate Prairie Road). Turn right at the fork and proceed 8 miles to the trailhead.

The **Mystic Trailhead** can also be reached from Hill City. Take FR 17 northwest for 5 miles until it intersects with Forest Road 231. Go 5.9 miles to the Mystic Trailhead, on the left.

Take US 385 north from Hill City for 18 miles until it intersects with County Road 299 (also Silver City Road and Forest Road 141). Follow this road 0.25 mile to the **Deer Creek Trailhead.** This trailhead is common to both the Deerfield Trail and the Centennial Trail.

To get to the **Silver City Trailhead,** take US 385 north from Hill City for 18 miles to the sign for Silver City. Turn left and continue on CR299 for 5 miles to the trailhead, a total of 23 miles.

The hike description below starts at the Custer Trailhead.

The Hike

Completed in 1992, the Deerfield Trail is one of the Black Hills' most recent additions. Because elevation loss (or gain) along the route is substantial, the trail's entire 18 miles is most easily traveled by proceeding from west to east.

From the Custer Trailhead at Deerfield Lake, the Deerfield Trail's western terminus, the trail ascends and descends for about 2 miles through Reynolds Prairie, high

Often you'll be rewarded with a sun-drenched forest ▶
along the Deerfield Trail.

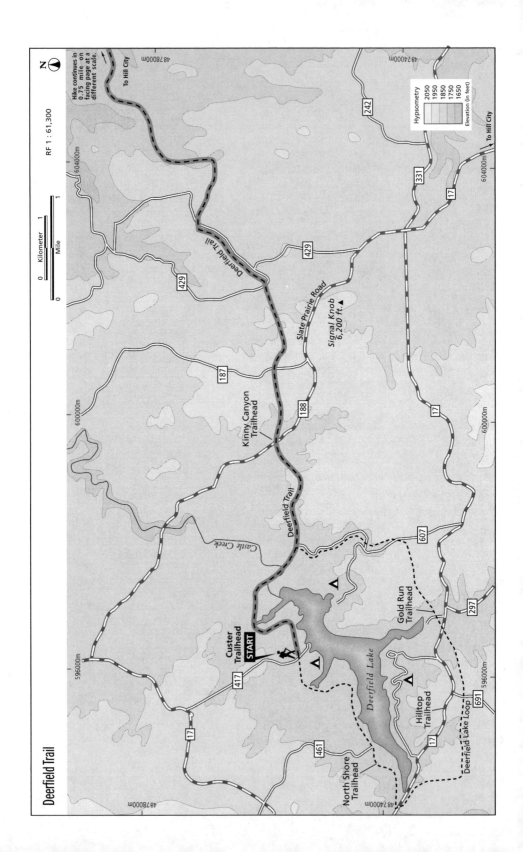

Deerfield Trail

RF 1 : 61,300

N

Hike continues in 0.75 mile on facing page at a different scale.

To Hill City

0   Kilometer   1
0   Mile   1

Hypsometry
2050
1950
1850
1750
1650
Elevation (in feet)

To Hill City

Deerfield Trail

Slate Prairie Road

Signal Knob
6,200 ft.

Kinny Canyon
Trailhead

Castle Creek

Deerfield Trail

Custer
Trailhead
START

Deerfield Lake

Gold Run
Trailhead

Hilltop
Trailhead

North Shore
Trailhead

Deerfield Lake Loop

604000m

600000m

596000m

604000m

600000m

596000m

4878000m

4874000m

4878000m

4874000m

417

17

461

17

691

17

297

607

17

331

242

188

187

429

429

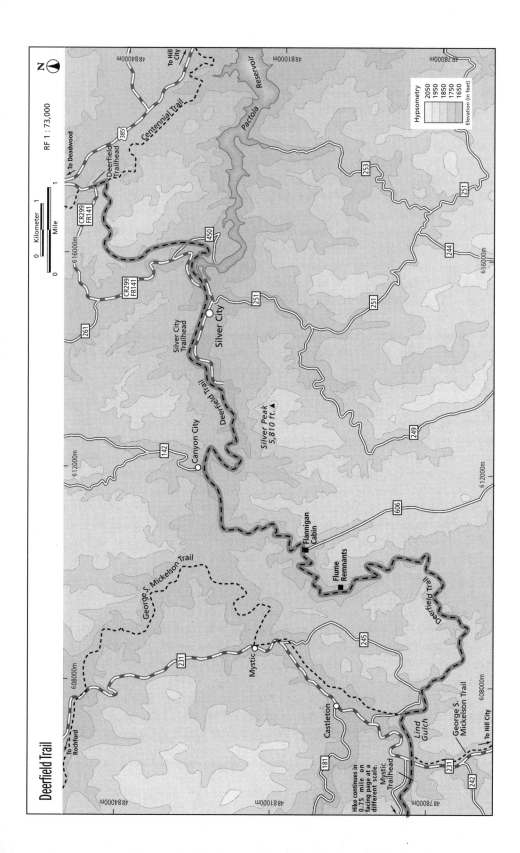

Deerfield Trail

RF 1 : 73,000

N

Hypsometry

2050
1950
1850
1750
1650

Elevation (in feet)

0   Kilometer   1
0   Mile   1

To Deadwood

To Hill City

385

Centennial Trail

Deerfield Trailhead

CR299 FR141

261

CR299 FR141

450

Silver City Trailhead

Silver City

251

251

Pactola Reservoir

253

251

244

Deerfield Trail

142

Canyon City

Silver Peak
5,810 ft. ▲

249

606

Flannigan Cabin

Flume Remnants

Deerfield Trail

George S. Mickelson Trail

231

Mystic

245

Lind Gulch

George S. Mickelson Trail

To Hill City

Castleton

Deerfield Trail

To Rochford

181

Mystic Trailhead

231

242

Hike continues in 0.75 mile on facing page at a different scale.

484000m

481000m

478000m

616000m

612000m

608000m

above the lake. It then passes the Kinny Canyon Trailhead at mile 3, concluding its climb at Slate Prairie and nearby Signal Knob, which at an elevation of 6,200 feet is the highest point along the Deerfield Trail. Here, the trail passes through a gate as the vegetation changes from ponderosa to a prairie ecosystem. Deer often graze in the meadows of Slate Prairie, and it's worth pausing to examine the grassy swales for movement.

The trail crosses a road 0.1 mile later and offers a brief view of Harney Peak, some 14 miles to the southeast. The trail then descends to a small creek and reenters the forest, which in places has been recently logged. The trail then climbs once again, though its general trend is always down.

The trail begins a rather abrupt descent 3.5 miles later as it enters Whitetail Gulch. Simultaneously the trail parallels Crooked Creek—flanked by stands of quaking aspen—where it soon intersects with the spur from the Mystic Trailhead. Just north are the Castleton dredge mining sites and Mystic, a mining camp turned railroad town. To the south is the old Mystic Civilian Conservation Corps camp, active in the 1930s.

At the Mystic Trailhead the trail crosses FR 231 and follows it for about 0.25 mile to the George S. Mickelson Trail. The Deerfield Trail then veers from the Mickelson Trail and climbs a four-wheel-drive trace, passes through a fence, and continues ascending through a stand of aspen until, at last, it crests.

The trail then drops through Lind Gulch. Here the vegetation changes to ponderosa and soon enters the sheer-walled canyon of Slate Creek Canyon, through which the trail passes for almost 3 miles. The entire trail to this point has been ideal for both hikers and mountain bikes, but this is one 1-mile stretch where hiking is much preferred. Cyclists must carry their bikes over rocks and, in one place, hoist them up rock outcroppings. Although the Forest Service has placed more than thirty flattened-log bridges here, high water takes its toll, forcing travelers to sometimes wade. (Other than a few segments of the trail in Slate Creek Canyon, the trail is appropriate for both hikers and cyclists, the latter of whom seem to dominate. Cyclists should remember when descending to maintain control, not only for their own safety but for that of slower hikers as well.)

In addition to being an extraordinarily beautiful canyon, Slate Creek serves as a prime fishery. Hikers would do well to pack a tent and fishing rod and spend several hours or days matching wits with the elusive brown trout here. When not involved in quality angling, history buffs will enjoy investigating the background of deteriorating cabins. As you travel you'll pass Black Tom Mine, Flannigan Cabin, and the Warren-Lamb flume, which in 1920 carried logs to the Canyon City railhead. Despite time, some of these structures remain in exceptional condition, and the Forest Service asks travelers to leave them as they find them.

About 6 miles beyond the Mystic Trailhead, Slate Creek converges with Castle Creek, and the two are redesignated Rapid Creek. From this point to the Silver City Trailhead, the going is fairly easy. By now the Deerfield Trail has descended to just over 4,600 feet and it is broad and flat. Bridges here are planked and broad for greater crossing ease. Fishing in some of the rocky canyons and their deep holes along Rapid Creek is excellent. The Forest Service has designated the segment as a walk-in fishery only.

Once this portion of the trail was traversed by the Rapid City, Black Hills & Western railway, which crossed more than a hundred bridges on its way to Mystic. The rails have been removed, making the segment of the trail along Rapid Creek to Silver City ideal for hikers, cyclists, and cross-country skiers.

From the Silver City trailhead, the canyon widens and begins a 2.5-mile climb. Finally the Deerfield Trail links up with the Centennial Trail at the Deer Creek trailhead, some 18 miles from where it originated.

Miles and Directions

0.0 Start from the Custer Trailhead.

2.0 Arrive at Signal Knob.

7.0 Pass the Mystic trailhead.

14.0 The going gets easier after Rapid Creek.

15.5 Arrive at Silver City.

18.0 End up at the Deer Creek trailhead at CR299/FR141.

35 Deerfield Lake Loop

A winding loop trail that begins in a prairie and meanders through ponderosa-pine forests as it circles Deerfield Lake.

Start: From the Custer Trailhead on the north shore of Deerfield Lake.
Distance: 10-mile loop.
Approximate hiking time: Most of a day.
Difficulty: Moderate to strenuous.
Highest elevation: 6,220 feet.
Seasons: Best from late spring through fall.
Other trail users: Horses, mountain bikers.
Land status: Black Hills National Forest.

Fees and permits: N/A
Maps: Black Hills National Forest Map, available for purchase at Forest Service offices and visitor centers; Forest Service Maps No. 40 and 40L, free from Forest Service offices and visitor centers.
Trail contact: Black Hills National Forest Visitor Center, 23939 U.S. Highway 385, Hill City, SD 57745; (605) 343-8755.

Finding the trailhead: To access the Custer Trailhead on the north shore of Deerfield Lake, proceed west from Hill City on Forest Road 17 (Deerfield Road) for 20 miles until the road intersects with Forest Road 417. Follow FR 417 several miles to the sign for Custer Campground. The Deerfield Lake Loop can also be accessed from the North Shore trailhead on the northwest end of Forest Road 461; from the Hilltop trailhead on the southern side of the lake; and from the Gold Run trailhead, 1 mile east of Hilltop trailhead on FR 17.

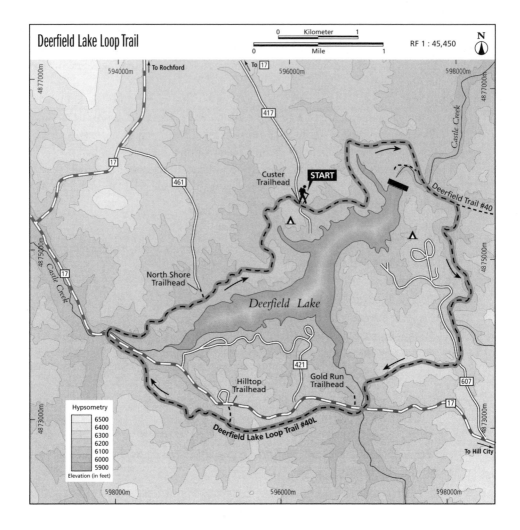

Deerfield Lake Loop Trail

0 Kilometer 1

0 Mile 1

RF 1 : 45,450

N

To Rochford

To 17

594000m

596000m

598000m

417

17

461

Custer
Trailhead

START

Deerfield Trail #40

North Shore
Trailhead

Deerfield Lake

Hypsometry

6500
6400
6300
6200
6100
6000
5900

Elevation (in feet)

Hilltop
Trailhead

421

Gold Run
Trailhead

Deerfield Lake Loop Trail #40L

607

17

To Hill City

598000m

596000m

598000m

The Hike

We began by hiking clockwise from the Custer Trailhead at the Custer Campground (also the western terminus of Deerfield Trail #40). The somewhat rocky trail begins as a progression of sharp, short ascents and descents through the southern end of Reynolds Prairie, passing through three cattle gates. In summer various wildflowers bloom. Because this is a multiple-use area, many gates are encountered throughout the hike. Be sure to leave them as they are, open or closed.

For the next 1.5 miles, you follow both Trails #40 and #40L; symbols for both routes are displayed. Signs shaped like deer prints signify Deerfield Trail #40; signs showing a lake engulfed by undulating waves signifies Deerfield Lake Loop #40L in the open areas. In wooded areas, follow the gray diamonds nailed on trees.

Approximately 1.5 miles from the trailhead, descend steeply onto a dirt road. Here you have the option of detouring for a short side trip to the right for 0.25 mile to the top of Deerfield Dam, banked 171 feet above the level of the nearby Castle Creek streambed. Back on the trail and three narrow, ankle-deep stream crossings later, travelers reach the junction of Trails #40 and #40L. Take 40L, which juts to the right, heading south.

Until this point lake views are numerous, but from here, those vistas become fewer as one begins to progress in a somewhat constant series of ups and downs through the ponderosa-pine forest. Quiet and lucky hikers often catch views of wildlife amidst the huge trees. About 3 miles into the hike, the trail crosses directly over a dirt road, Forest Road 607. The narrow path swings west, still in the forest. About 0.75 mile later, after a steep descent offering a great lake view (near Gold Run trailhead), you will cross FR 17 to the south side, directly opposite a private campground. Go through the gate (you might have to crawl over or under) to pick up the trail, which then parallels the highway for about 2 miles, heading west. Hilltop trailhead is located here on the north side of the highway.

Following the signs, you must then cross back over FR 17, where a small footbridge takes you over Castle Creek. The fishing here is supposed to be good. The final 2.5 to 3 miles assume a series of steep ups and downs around the northwest side of the lake, winding high on dirt cliffs and passing through woods and open fields until the trail concludes on the gravel road just outside Custer Campground.

Miles and Directions

0.0 Start at the Custer Trailhead at the Custer Campground on the north shore of Deerfield Lake. Hike the trail clockwise.

1.5 Take side trail to visit the top of Deerfield Dam.

3.75 Cross paved FR 17.

6.5 A small footbridge takes you over Castle Creek.

10.0 The loop ends on the road just outside Custer Campground.

36 Flume Trail

A fascinating trek through one of the historic gold-mining areas in the Black Hills. The trail follows, in part, an old flume bed, and there are good interpretive descriptions throughout. If you hike the entire length, you'll need to arrange for a shuttle or for a two-car system.

Start: From the western terminus of the Flume Trail, called the Calumet trailhead. Go to Sheridan Lake Campground and follow signs to the trail on the southeast shore of the lake.
Distance: 11 miles one-way.
Approximate hiking time: All day, or an easy 2-day trek.
Difficulty: Easy to moderate.
Highest elevation: 5,300 feet.
Seasons: Best from late spring through fall.

Land status: Black Hills National Forest.
Fees and permits: N/A
Maps: Black Hills National Forest Map, available for purchase at Forest Service offices and at visitor centers; USDA Forest Service Flume Trail No. 50 map, free at Forest Service offices and Black Hills visitor centers.
Trail contact: Black Hills National Forest Visitor Center, 23939 U.S. Highway 385, Hill City, SD 57745; (605) 343-8755.

Finding the trailhead: Take US 385 north from the center of Hill City for 6 miles to Sheridan Lake Campground on the right. Go through the entrance gate and follow the signs for the Flume Trail and Centennial Trail trailheads on the southeast shore of the lake. This is the western terminus of the Flume Trail and is called the Calumet trailhead. The eastern terminus, Coon Hollow trailhead, is 0.25 mile from the old mining town of Rockerville, located on Forest Road 233, which is about 16 miles northeast of Hill City off U.S. Highway 16 east.

The Hike

The Flume Trail is filled with the history of gold mining in the area and is, in addition, a wonderful nature walk. One of two National Recreation Trails in Black Hills National Forest, the path follows much of an old flume bed. Old parts of the wooden flume can still be seen along this route, as can other historic artifacts. Many photo opportunities exist on this trail, including canyons, forests, tunnels, and prairie fields alive with wildflowers in summer. Hikers can't help but imagine the gold miners who built the flume with picks, hammers, and shovels.

Visitors can hike this trail in one day or make it a comfortable two-day hike. You can camp anywhere as long as you are at least 100 feet off the nearest trail or road. Those desiring to hike the entire length of trail one-way should arrange for a shuttle. Those wishing to backtrack or hike shorter segments can access the trail from two other trailheads, the Upper Spring Creek Trailhead (about 1 mile east of Calumet Trailhead) or the Boulder Hill Trailhead (about 2.75 miles from the trail's eastern terminus).

From the parking lot at Sheridan Lake, the trail begins by crossing a small footbridge over a clear feeder creek. Flume Trail #50 shares this easy, relatively flat walk

Flume Trail; Spring Creek Loop; Boulder Hill

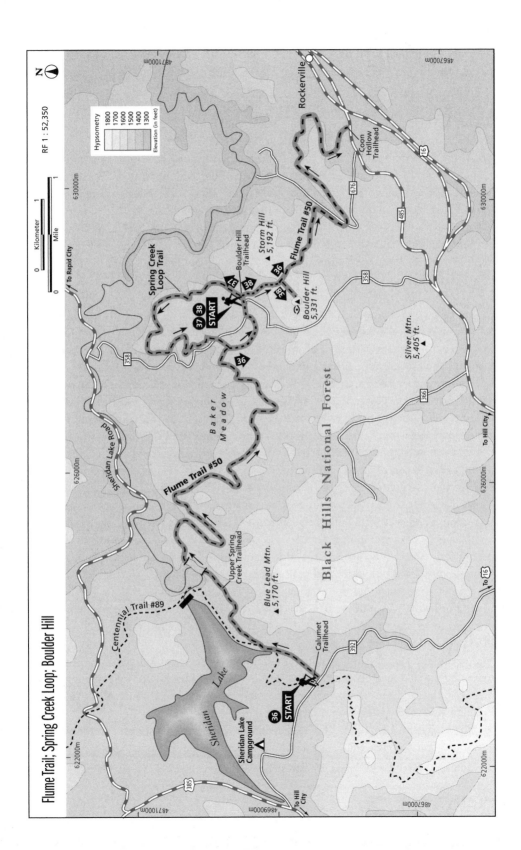

with the Centennial Trail #89 for about 1 mile. Together they parallel the lakeshore as they head toward the east end of the lake and the earthen dam. Upon reaching the dam, #89 heads north; about 20 feet prior to that, the Flume Trail #50 cuts sharply to the east (right) into pine forest. The trail markers on brown posts are a distinctive red, white, and blue, signifying you are hiking a National Recreation Trail. At this first junction, hikers ascend to the ridge above the dam.

At the next interpretive sign, you have the option of going north (right) to the Upper Spring Creek Trailhead (which is also a walk-in fishing area) or continuing straight on the Flume Trail #50. Continue walking along a cliff base above a boulder field for about 1.5 miles in from the trailhead, where you'll reach the first of two old tunnels on the trail. Very low and cut entirely by hand and back muscle into ancient rock, this tunnel extends for 75 to 100 feet. Hikers who have an aversion to dark, low places have the option of hiking over the top. The trail then begins to swing away from the canyon.

At mile 2, the path ascends and descends briefly in a small series of switchbacks through the ponderosa woods. Soon you encounter the first of many signs along the trail that interpret the Rockerville Flume, vital to the area's gold-mining operations in the late 1800s. The path then ascends out of Blue Lead Draw to Spring Creek Canyon. The creek can be heard 140 feet below as it rushes into the lake.

Continuing on the Flume Trail #50, the second tunnel is soon reached, this one about 25 feet long. The trail then swings due south for 0.5 mile, descends to cross a feeder creek, then ascends gently to the north. At this point you will pick up the first of many old four-wheel-drive trails that the Flume Trail #50 follows. Ascend through a flower-strewn meadow to the Baker Meadow overview, which offers a prime example of a prairie and forest edging. An "edge" is an ecological term indicating an area wildlife prefers because of the juxtaposition of food and cover.

At this point you are 4.25 miles west of Boulder Hill, and this massive rocky hill (elevation 5,331 feet) can easily be seen to the east on clear days. The trail makes another series of gently rolling descents and ascents in meadows and woods, on and off old four-wheel-drive roads. Until this point the trail has been well marked, but 1.5 miles west of the Boulder Hill trailhead, it can become confusing. Trail markers are often absent, but some FOOT TRAVEL ONLY signs exist. Follow these as the trail heads north for 0.75 mile then swings southeast for another 0.75 mile, at which point it crosses, then parallels, Forest Road 358 and leads to the Boulder Hill trailhead parking lot.

Leaving the Boulder Hill trailhead, the trail proceeds east and slightly southeast, following the trail markers and FOOT TRAVEL ONLY signs. For the first mile or so, you may have to search out the signs a bit, but the final 2 miles to Coon Hollow trailhead are well marked and have interpretive signs along the way.

The trail is broader toward the end as it winds through the forests. Hikers pass over a rock cut, through which the flume water flowed, dug by hand. One of the last interpretive signs informs travelers that they've reached the downstream terminus of the flume. Upon reaching Coon Hollow trailhead (the eastern terminus of the Flume Trail), the town of Rockerville (population: twenty) is about 0.75 mile west.

Miles and Directions

0.0 Start at the western terminus, the Calumet trailhead. The Flume Trail #50 shares the beginning of this walk with the Centennial Trail #89 for about 1 mile.

1.0 The Flume Trail #50 cuts sharply right (east); take this turn. The Centennial Trail #89 goes north. Do not follow the Centennial Trail.

2.0 Arrive at the first tunnel.

2.2 Arrive at the second tunnel.

3.0 The Baker Meadow overlook offers fine views of prairie and forest edging.

7.0 Linger at the Boulder Hill trailhead. It's also the location of Spring Creek Loop Trail and Boulder Hill.

11.0 Arrive at the eastern trail terminus, Coon Hollow trailhead.

OPTION: At mile 7.0 hikers have the option of taking an extra half-hour hike to the top of Boulder Hill (leave time to linger there) and/or hike the easy 3-mile Spring Creek Loop Trail, before completing the last few miles of the Flume Trail #50.

Located south of Spring Creek Loop and the Boulder Hill trailhead, the Boulder Hill Trail is short, steep, and well worth the effort. A marker adjacent to the Spring Creek Loop Trail points the way around the base of Boulder Hill to the east side, where a narrow trail then ascends quite steeply for several hundred feet to the summit. Retrace your route back to the trailhead.

37 Spring Creek Loop

A flat loop trail through woods on a ridge above Spring Creek, which can be included as an addition to the Flume Trail or simply hiked on its own.

See map on page 119
Start: From the Boulder Hill trailhead, which is approximately the midsection of the Flume Trail #50 (off Forest Road 358).
Distance: 3-mile loop.
Approximate hiking time: 1 to 2 hours.
Difficulty: Easy.
Seasons: Best from late spring through fall.
Other trail users: Hikers only.
Land status: Black Hills National Forest.

Fees and permits: N/A
Maps: Black Hills National Forest Map, available for purchase at Forest Service offices and at visitor centers; USDA Forest Service Map No. 50 (Flume Trail) free at Forest Service offices and Black Hills visitor centers.
Trail contact: Black Hills National Forest Visitor Center, 23939 U.S. Highway 385, Hill City, SD 57745; (605) 343-8755.

Finding the trailhead: Spring Creek Loop Trail is accessed from the Boulder Hill trailhead, which is considered the midsection of the Flume Trail #50. From Hill City take U.S. Highway 16 east for 11.1 miles to FR 358 on the left of the highway. Follow this dirt road for 2.3 miles to the trailhead.

The Hike

Part of the Flume Creek National Recreation Trail, Spring Creek Loop Trail is marked by the distinctive red, white, and blue NRT markers on posts for the first 2 miles. The path is marked for foot travel only.

From the trailhead parking lot, we hiked counterclockwise, following the sign for Spring Creek Loop to the north. The trail immediately parallels an old road that is obviously intended to be returned to a natural condition and that passes huge piles of old wood. A comfortable, wide forest path, the Spring Creek Loop Trail meanders along a cliff edge and through stands of ponderosa pine.

At about 1 mile an interpretive sign informs you that you're standing on an old flume bed, 300 feet above Spring Creek. Spring Creek is a great trout stream, but too difficult to reach from this trail. There are other access sites, such as Spring Creek Canyon, below Sheridan Lake. Parallel the creek—which you'll hear more than you'll see—for another 0.5 mile. The trail then begins to wind south.

Hike another 0.5 mile and you'll see rocky and woody remnants of the old flume. But here the trail can become a bit indistinct. Continue walking south, following signs that say FOOT TRAVEL ONLY, and you will soon cross the dirt FR 358. The trail parallels the road for several hundred yards, crosses FR 358 once more, then returns to the trailhead.

Miles and Directions

0.0 Start at the Boulder Hill Trailhead, midway along the Flume Trail #50. Head north, in a counterclockwise direction.

1.0 An interpretive sign informs you that you're standing on an old flume bed.

2.5 Cross FR 358.

2.7 Cross back over FR 358.

3.0 Reach the Boulder Hill Trailhead and completion of the loop.

38 Boulder Hill

A short but steep ascent (a twenty- to thirty-minute hike) to the top of a high, rocky outcropping, offering dramatic views.

See map on page 119
Start: From the Boulder Hill Trailhead along the Flume Trail #50.
Distance: 2 miles out and back.
Approximate hiking time: 20 to 30 minutes actual hiking time.
Difficulty: Strenuous.
Highest elevation: 5,331 feet.
Seasons: Best from late spring through fall.

Other trail users: Hikers only.
Land status: Black Hills National Forest.
Fees and permits: N/A
Maps: Free Forest Service brochure of Flume Trail (FS No. 50); Black Hills National Forest map.
Trail contact: Black Hills National Forest Visitor Center, 23939 U.S. Highway 385, Hill City, SD 57745; (605) 343-8755.

Finding the trailhead: Boulder Hill is accessed from the Boulder Hill trailhead, considered the midsection of the Flume Trail #50. From Hill City take U.S. Highway 16 east for 11.1 miles to Forest Road 358 on the left of the highway. Follow this dirt road for 2.3 miles to the trailhead.

The Hike

Boulder Hill is one of the special features found along the Flume Trail #50 and makes another nice side trip on the Flume Trail #50 hike—or a good jaunt just for its own sake. Located south of Spring Creek Loop and the Boulder Hill Trailhead, this short, steep spur hike is well worth the effort. Upon reaching the 5,331-foot summit, we agreed that it would be a perfect vision-quest spot, in addition to being a photographer's dream.

A marker adjacent to the Spring Creek Loop Trail points the way around the base of Boulder Hill to the east side, where a narrow trail then ascends quite steeply for several hundred feet through the craggy rocks to the summit. Hikers can alternately locate the primitive old road on the west side and take that up— we found the old road rather difficult to follow, so we opted for the marked trail. Because forest roads surround Boulder Hill, getting lost is difficult—so plain bushwhacking is also an option.

From the peak, the sensational 360-degree vistas include the Badlands, rolling prairies, the Needles formations, and Harney Peak.

39 Bear Mountain Ski Trails

Two high–mountain loop trails affording hikers and mountain bikers with extraordinary views and a great diversity of vegetation and wildlife.

Start: From the Medicine Mountain Boy Scout Camp. Signs for the camp are found along U.S. Highway 16, north of Custer, South Dakota.
Distance: 9.0-mile loop.
Approximate hiking time: Half a day.
Difficulty: Easy to moderately strenuous.
Highest elevation: 7,153 feet.
Seasons: Year-round.
Other trail users: Mountain bikers, horses, skiers.

Land status: Black Hills National Forest.
Fees and permits: N/A
Maps: Black Hills National Forest Map, available for purchase at Forest Service offices and visitor centers; USDA Forest Service Map of Bear Mountain Trails No. 23 and 25, free at Forest Service offices and Black Hills visitor centers.
Trail contact: Black Hills National Forest Visitor Center, 23939 U.S. Highway 385, Hill City, SD 57745; (605) 343-8755.

Finding the trailhead: The trails are accessed from Medicine Mountain Boy Scout Camp, which is located southwest of Hill City and northwest of the town of Custer. Signs pointing you in the right direction for the camp are found on US 16. From Custer, South Dakota, proceed as follows: Take US 385/16 north for approximately 4 miles. Take County Road 297 northwest for approximately 8 miles, then follow Forest Road 299 (Bobcat Road) north for 3 to 4 miles to the Boy Scout Camp.

The Hike

The Forest Service is justifiably proud of the Bear Mountain Ski Trails and hope they will be used more frequently by hikers and mountain bikers. Bear Mountain is one of the highest mountains in the Black Hills at 7,153 feet. At its peak is a fire tower, one of the principal towers in the area. For hikers on Bear Mountain trails, the 400-yard spur off XC25 to the lookout offers views that are breathtaking. The other vantage point at the Grand Vista Overlook (7,040 feet) is equally spectacular, offering views of Harney Peak, Little Devils Tower, the Cathedral Spires, and many other landmarks. This overlook is also on a spur trails off XC25.

Certainly one of the best reasons to hike these trails is the varied scenery. The trails wind through draws, pass through pine and spruce forests, skirt stands of aspen, and travel along a limestone rim. Wildlife is abundant in this area. According to Bear Mountain trail personnel, mountain lions occasionally are seen. Elk and deer abound; coyotes, grouse, and wild turkeys are sometimes glimpsed.

The Medicine Mountain Boy Scout Camp serves as the trailhead for both trails. It's perfectly all right to park overnight there, and restroom facilities are available. We recommend the XC25 loop at 9.0 miles long, including the spur trails.

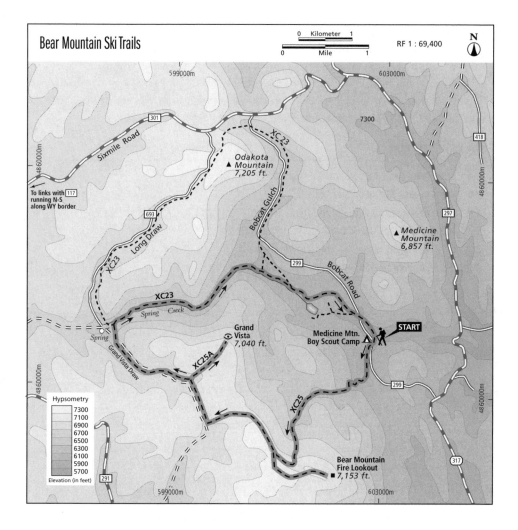

Bear Mountain Ski Trails

Odakota Mountain 7,205 ft.

Medicine Mountain 6,857 ft.

Grand Vista 7,040 ft.

Medicine Mtn. Boy Scout Camp

START

Bear Mountain Fire Lookout 7,153 ft.

To links with 117 running N-S along WY border

Sixmile Road

Long Draw

Bobcat Gulch

Bobcat Road

XC23

Spring Creek

Spring

Grand Vista Draw

XC25A

XC25

Hypsometry

7300
7100
6900
6700
6500
6300
6100
5900
5700

Elevation (in feet)

RF 1 : 69,400

Kilometer

Mile

N

Beginning on the southern route of XC25, hikers ascend 1,000 feet in about 2 miles to Bear Mountain. To visit the fire tower, the spur trail here is only 0.5 mile. Return to XC25 and follow the limestone rim to the spur trail XC25A, which heads northeast for 0.8 mile to the Grand Vista Overlook. The name says it all: From here you can see more than thirty mountain peaks.

Return to XC25 and head northwest down Grand Vista Draw. XC25 concludes 1 mile from here, at the intersection with XC23. By heading east on XC23, you can make a loop, traveling down Spring Creek and returning to the trailhead from which you started.

Our trail profile delineates XC25 and XC23, combining to make the shorter loop of the two. The trails are well marked by signs with a bear claw in a square indicating the ski trail. In densely wooded areas, blue diamond blazes are used.

The free trail brochure available from the Forest Service notes segments of both trails that are used by snowmobilers during the winter season. Drinking water is not available on the trails. Be sure to purify any stream or spring water you use.

For a very long hike, you can continue north on XC23 up Long Draw. By doing this, you follow the perimeter of the loop trails, making a one- or two-day hike of some 16 miles. Or hike the northern loop, XC23, a 9.45-mile trip.

Miles and Directions

0.0 Start at Medicine Mountain Boy Scout Camp.

2.0 Visit the Bear Mountain Fire Lookout.

4.0 Arrive at the spur trail to Grand Vista.

5.7 This is the end of XC25. Turn east (right) onto XC23.

8.0 Stay to the right to continue back to the trailhead.

9.0 Return to Medicine Mountain Boy Scout Camp.

Additional Hikes

Veterans Point

Those who seek views and easy walking can take the barrier-free, 0.5-mile Veterans Point trail around a point overlooking Pactola Reservoir. The paved walk at Veterans Point is open year-round. There is also a short one-way spur trail of 1,200 feet off the loop. The grade on the trail is 6 percent, which can be somewhat challenging for visitors in wheelchairs. There are curbs and railings along the trail, however. The path loops around a point, offering wonderful views of Pactola Reservoir, the rocky shoreline, and the hills surrounding the area.

To reach the trailhead from Hill City, take U.S. Highway 385 north for approximately 16 miles to Pactola Visitor Center on Pactola Reservoir. The Veterans Point walk is located about 1 mile north of the visitor center on US 385 at the northeast end of the reservoir and the dam.

Aspen Leaf

Another short (0.25-mile) interpretive trail is located at the Pactola Visitor Center. The first portion of the Aspen Leaf Trail is barrier-free, but the trail ranges from easy to strenuous. This interpretive trail was designed to show and identify several regional species of plants and trees. The trail begins as a paved observation sidewalk that goes around the backside of the visitor center, offering great views of Pactola Reservoir. This portion of the walk is barrier-free with a 5 percent slope. The trail then leads downhill on a series of steps to an observation deck. From here, walkers can proceed downhill even farther, to the edge of the reservoir.

The trail begins and ends at the Pactola Visitor Center on Pactola Reservoir, 16 miles north of Hill City on U.S. Highway 385.

Wind Cave
National Park

L ate one July afternoon we sat on Boland Ridge looking west over a broad expanse of land known as Red Valley. Below us in the distance, large black dots quickly assumed the distinct and recognizable forms of bison. Mating season was at its height, and several of the bulls had not yet determined their order of dominance. They were angry and were fighting in earnest.

Raising our binoculars, we watched as two gigantic bulls galloped side by side. Suddenly one of them stopped and wheeled. The two collided, but with no apparent ill effect. Red dust rose around the two, as they began raking one another with their daggerlike horns. Within a minute, the battle was over. Just what these two giants had concluded was unclear, but for no apparent reason the fighting ceased and the two began grazing in the tall prairie grasses, seemingly oblivious to one another.

We sat on the ridge watching for more than an hour as similar battles continued. The setting was a primordial one, a scene from historic times. Then, with little warning, a violent afternoon storm blew in. For ten minutes wind, rain, and hail assaulted us. When it ended, only the hushed breath of the prairie breeze stirred the grasses. Not a single bison dotted the landscape, and the silence was immense. Seldom had we been more moved by the utter magnificence of nature—the staggering beauty of the prairie and its life, which we were to experience over and over as we hiked the trails of Wind Cave National Park.

Wind Cave dates back 320 million years, making it one of the world's oldest caverns. The cave system contains fascinating and rare formations as well. Inside this cave, viewers are presented with sights of rare beauty. Wind Cave has one of the largest displays of "boxwork": a fragile lattice formation made of calcite, which adorns the cave walls and ceilings. Other rare formations contained in the cave include "frostwork" and "helictite bushes," whose names are suggestive of their looks. The cave contains but few stalactites and stalagmites.

Paha Sapa limestone provides the basis for these formations created by the action of water on soft rock over millions of years. The waters that seeped into the cave did

Watch where you sit. Prickly pear cactus is abundant.

not flow through but sat stagnant, aiding in the dissolving of Wind Cave's limestone into many passageways. Ancient teepee rings near the cave testify that Native Americans knew a cave existed here, though anthropologists believe the area's earliest peoples refrained from explorations, believing that spirits lurked underground.

The first white settlers to explore the cave were the brothers Jesse and Tom Bingham, who in 1881 heard strange whistling sounds emanating from the earth. The sounds drew them to the hole, which they then showed to others. Nine years later regular public tours began, which visited many of the same rooms viewed by tour groups today. On one wall in the Garden of Eden section of the cave, eight explorers left their signatures adjacent to the date "8-17-1892." The writing remains as part of the cave's history. In the one hundred–plus years since the cave's discovery, spelunkers have explored and mapped more than 117 miles of the cave's complex system. Managers estimate that the figure represents only 5 percent of the total cave and that literally hundreds of miles remain uncharted. Today we realize that changes in barometric pressure affect the intake or outflow of air from the cave. The flow creates the steady whistling noises that attracted the Binghams.

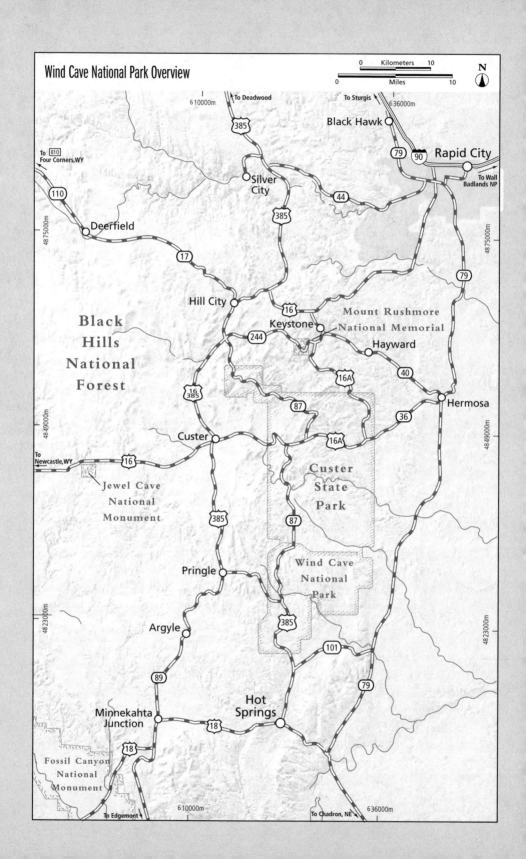

Recognizing the cave's extraordinary features—as well as the extraordinarily beautiful prairie ecosystem above it—Congress sought protection of the Wind Cave complex, and in 1903 Wind Cave became our seventh national park. Since that time, managers have eliminated solo and private cave explorations, primarily for safety reasons but also for protection of the cave. Groups of cave enthusiasts called "grottos," with park permission and permits, explore and map uncharted sections of the cave. Cavers desiring to explore Wind Cave should contact one of the participating grottos. Otherwise, visitors may take one of the park-provided, year-round fee tours, led by park personnel who are fully trained in caving. Three tours are available in summer, each costing several dollars. In essence, these cave tours are short subterranean hikes, all of which depart from the Wind Cave Visitor Center.

No longer is it necessary to enter the hole used by early Wind Cave explorers, though you can still see the old entrance by following a trail from the visitor center. Simply follow the signs. Of the below-ground hikes, two (the Fairgrounds and the Natural Entrance Tours) are 0.5 mile long. A third, the Garden of Eden, is 0.25 mile. Hiking times for these tours vary from 1 to 1½ hours.

Additional special options are offered from June to August, such as the 1-mile Candlelight Tour, during which each visitor carries a candle lantern to illuminate the caverns. Another special event, called the Caving Tour, involves much crawling over a three- to four-hour period. Visitors need reservations and tickets for these tours, available at the visitor center.

After Labor Day the number of tours is reduced to one. Wind Cave offers the Garden of Eden Tour three times a day during the winter months. The Garden of Eden Tour lasts about one hour. An elevator plummets 110 feet (the equivalent of 11 stories) into the cave's depths. The water table is located many more feet down at 430 feet, 43 stories deep. Visitors on this tour step from the elevator into a natural, large cavern where tunnels lead off in many directions. The temperature is a constant fifty-three degrees throughout the cave, and the humidity varies between 90 and 100 percent. Visitors view the "popcorn" formations as well as "boxwork," as fragile as it is rare. You'll learn that cave walls should never be touched, since oils from our skin can damage the formations and stop their growth.

For added fun, the tour guide shuts off the cave electricity—warning visitors in advance. Many people are rendered speechless. An unearthly quiet cloaks the group, and a darkness blacker than any night descends. At last (after maybe sixty seconds) the naturalist strikes a match and lights a candle lantern made from an old lard bucket. Everyone gasps. The demonstration suggests how early cave explorers found their way through the eerie dark mazes. The tour is well suited for families. It is fun and informative, offering glimpses of the incredible beauty that is Wind Cave below the ground.

Though the park is better known for its miles of explored underground passages, park visitors can also explore Wind Cave above the ground, in one of the nation's lushest and most pristine prairie grasslands. Here, above the nation's fifth-longest underground passageway, exists an incredible prairie ecosystem and ponderosa-pine forest that includes a diverse mix of wildlife roaming freely throughout the park's 28,295 acres. Because motorized vehicles and mountain bikes are confined to the park's roads, hikers who venture onto the park's 30 miles of trails are generally rewarded with unparalleled sightings of wildlife. You'll see firsthand many of the same grassland conditions that Black Hills pioneers saw in the 1890s.

To keep its environment pristine, Wind Cave has been designated an "indicator park." Researchers here are evaluating the past effects that climate and fire have played on grassland ecology. Look for the small tracts of fenced enclosures intended to exclude bison, elk, deer, and pronghorn antelope. By examining the vegetation inside the fence and comparing it to vegetative growth outside, biologists can monitor the impact of grazing on hardwood species such as aspen, ash, willow, and chokecherry. In this way, scientists hope to better determine the carrying capacity (what they eat and how much) of the park's hoofed animals.

Hikers will also see trees, snags, and stumps that have a wedge or cross section cut into them. The marks indicate that biologists have been evaluating the age of the park's trees and forests to determine how often fires burned throughout the area. The information tells biologists how often they should conduct their program of prescribed burning. In the historic past, fires were an integral part of prairie ecology. Without fires, ponderosa pine would soon replace the lush grasslands hikers now encounter.

Wind Cave National Park offers eleven maintained trails, three of which are interpretive self-guided trails. You also can combine several trails to make nice, logistically workable loops. With the exception of the Boland Ridge Trail, none of the hikes in this area is very steep; even Boland ascends but a few hundred feet. Several of the longer hikes in Wind Cave National Park require effort simply because the trails wind through the prairie lands for several miles and are at times faint. Once four-wheel-drive roads, these trails can be easily confused with game trails.

If you find yourself lost on one of these routes, hike to a high point and search for landmarks such as a fire tower or nearby road. One ranger/naturalist says that because landmarks are generally visible, Wind Cave National Park provides an excellent setting to refine map-reading skills. Triangulate from the landmark to pinpoint your location and the lost trail. Anticipate confusion by allowing for additional time afield, and remember to carry the following:

1. More water than you think you'll need (and on some summer days it still might not be enough). For a full day's outing in the summer, carry 1 gallon per person.
2. Binoculars.
3. Compass and topo map. National Geographic/Trails Illustrated Topo Map No. 238 contains all park trails.
4. Hat and sunscreen.
5. Sturdy boots.
6. Tick and bug spray in spring and summer.

Much of the park's northwest is designated as a backcountry camping area. No open fires are allowed. If you need a fire to cook, you must carry a backpacker stove. Additionally, you must obtain a free backcountry use permit from the visitor center or at one of the Centennial Trail trailheads; must camp 0.25 mile from any road and out of sight of any trails; be 100 feet from any water source; and treat all water before drinking. One final suggestion for summertime prairie hiking: Start early, not only to avoid the heat, but also to see the park's wild animals.

Though all trails expose you to the prairie ecosystem, each offers fresh perspectives. You simply can't go wrong spending several days hiking all 30 miles of the Wind Cave aboveground trails. Several people we met had hiked all the trails and now return summer after summer to do so again!

In 2003 paleontologists discovered the teeth of an ancient, thirty-two-million-year-old rhinoceros. The site has been designated as the Centennial Site. Other animal remains, such as a complete skull and part of a skeleton, were also found on the site. These discoveries have since been moved to the Mammoth Site in Hot Springs, but Wind Cave also has displays of these finds.

Wind Cave National Park is located in the southeast corner of the Black Hills, adjacent to Custer State Park on its north boundary and an hour and forty-five-minute drive south of Rapid City. Take South Dakota Highway 79 south out of Rapid City for 18 miles to Hermosa. From there follow South Dakota Highway 36 to Custer State Park, and take U.S. Highway 16A west through Custer State Park for 10 miles to South Dakota Highway 87. Follow SD 87 south for about 12 miles to the entrance to Wind Cave National Park. At this time Custer State Park does not charge a fee for those passing through the park to Wind Cave.

At the junction of SD 87 and U.S. Highway 385, take US 385 south to reach the park's visitor center. You can also access the park by following the "scenic route" of U.S. Highway 85, south from Interstate 90 between Spearfish and Sturgis. Follow US 85 south toward Deadwood, then take US 385 south through the center of the Black Hills until you reach Wind Cave National Park.

Hot Springs is an interesting, friendly little town in the southwest corner of South Dakota, from which you can easily reach Wind Cave National Park. Northbound travelers from Nebraska should take US 385 north through Hot Springs and on into the park. Southbound travelers from Rapid City should follow SD 79 south for 48 miles to U.S. Highway 18 west into Hot Springs, then follow US 385 into Wind Cave.

The trails in Wind Cave are all named. The park charges no entry fee. Elevation gain is generally so minimal that a description of such is not mentioned in the trail write-ups.

40 Cold Brook Canyon Trail

A scenic meander through a tallgrass prairie valley that simultaneously explores a canyon in southwest Wind Cave National Park.

Start: At the trailhead 1.5 miles south of the visitor center on U.S. Highway 385.
Distance: 2.8 miles out and back.
Approximate hiking time: 2 to 3 hours.
Difficulty: Easy.
Seasons: Best late spring through fall.
Other trail users: Hikers only.
Land status: Wind Cave National Park.

Fees and permits: N/A
Maps: National Geographic/Trails Illustrated topo map No. 238; free Park Service map and brochure of Wind Cave National Park available at the visitor center.
Trail contact: Wind Cave National Park, RR 1, Box 190, Hot Springs, SD 57747; (605) 745-4600; www.nps.gov/wica.

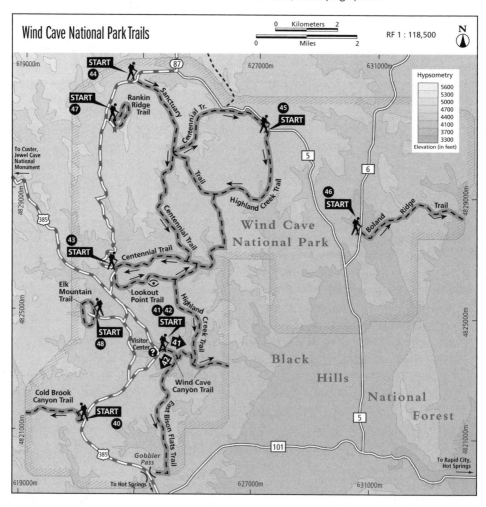

Finding the trailhead: The trail begins 1.5 miles south of the visitor center on US 385, on the right-hand (west) side of the road.

The Hike

The trail begins along an old road that gently descends into a tallgrass prairie valley flanked on one side by a small ridge of ponderosa. The well-marked trail is often frequented by bison—sometimes in summer, by lone males in rut. Be alert for them and also for rattlesnakes.

The trail proceeds west; shortly the canyon narrows and is further compressed by rock formations that play host to a variety of avian species, including prairie falcons. The trail concludes at a sturdy fence and helps mark the park's western boundary.

The ease of the hike and the abundance and variety of prairie grasses and birdlife combine to make this trail particularly appropriate for family outings.

41 Wind Cave Canyon Trail

A walk through Wind Cave Canyon, ending at the park boundary fence on the eastern side.

See map on page 134

Start: From the trailhead on the east side of U.S. Highway 385, 1 mile north of the southern entrance to the visitor center.

Distance: 3.6 miles out and back.

Approximate hiking time: 2 to 3 hours.

Difficulty: Easy.

Seasons: Best from spring through fall.

Other trail users: Hikers only.

Land status: Wind Cave National Park.

Fees and permits: N/A

Maps: National Geographic/Trails Illustrated topo map No. 238; free Park Service map and brochure of Wind Cave National Park available at the visitor center.

Trail contact: Wind Cave National Park, RR 1, Box 190, Hot Springs, SD 57747; (605) 745-4600; www.nps.gov/wica.

Finding the trailhead: This trail is located on the east side of US 385, 1 mile north of the southern entrance to the park's visitor center. Wind Cave Canyon Trail is also an access trail for two other trails, namely, East Bison Flats Trail and the Highland Creek Trail.

The Hike

Wind Cave National Park naturalists say this trail is an exceptionally good one for birding, since the abundant limestone cliffs provide nesting grounds for several species, including the great horned owl.

Buffalo wallows are numerous in Wind Cave National Park. Sweeping cloud formations characterize the summer sky.

42 East Bison Flats Trail

A prairie hike where wildlife is at times abundant.

See map on page 134
Start: At the northern end of the trailhead opposite the visitor center. You'll be starting on Wind Cave Canyon Trail.
Distance: 7.4 miles out and back.
Approximate hiking time: Plan on nearly a full day.
Difficulty: Moderately strenuous.
Seasons: Best from spring through fall.
Other trail users: Hikers only.

Land status: Wind Cave National Park.
Fees and permits: N/A
Maps: National Geographic/Trails Illustrated topo map No. 238; free Park Service map and brochure of Wind Cave National Park available at the visitor center.
Trail contact: Wind Cave National Park, RR 1, Box 190, Hot Springs, SD 57747; (605) 745–4600; www.nps.gov/wica.

Finding the trailhead: Depending on the direction from which you plan to hike, the trailhead is located either opposite the visitor center on U.S. Highway 385 (take Wind Cave Canyon Trail trailhead) or 3 miles south of the visitor center on US 385, at Gobbler Pass trailhead.

The Hike

This trail is mildly strenuous and well marked. From the northern end the trail proceeds southeast along Wind Cave Canyon Trail for 0.75 mile following an old road that winds through the canyon and offers a cool respite from the summer's prairie heat. Wind Cave Canyon Trail then intersects with East Bison Flats Trail. Take East Bison Flats, which climbs a short distance to the ridge then proceeds south. Here hikers are offered views to the north of Rankin Fire Tower.

Trail markers have been abundant to this point, but as you proceed through the grasslands, some are obscured by tall grasses or have been knocked down by bison. Appropriately, the park has named the prairie through which the trail proceeds Bison Flats. Bison wallows are numerous, and bones picked over by coyotes often litter the ground. Prairie dogs are also abundant. They keep the grass clipped short and stimulate new growth, much preferred by bison. Walk quietly and chances are good that you will see a fat coyote or herd of pronghorn antelope. Stay very alert for bison and for rattlesnakes, especially near prairie-dog towns.

About 0.75 mile after entering the grassland community, the trail ascends a small ridge. Keep left of the ponderosa forest. The boundary fence is to the east and often visible. The trail soon descends to a creek, then cuts sharply west. For the final 0.75 mile, parallel the fence and the road until you reach the southern trailhead, located at the end of the fence on US 385 at Gobbler Pass. From here you'll need to backtrack or meet a previously arranged shuttle back to your vehicle.

43 Lookout Point–Centennial Trail Loop

A loop hike that offers a chance to examine both prairie and riparian habitats.

See map on page 134
Start: At the Lookout Point/Centennial trailhead (they are one and the same) off South Dakota Highway 87.
Distance: 4-mile loop.
Approximate hiking time: 3 to 5 hours.
Difficulty: Easy to moderately strenuous.
Highest Elevation: 4,480 ft.
Seasons: Best from spring through fall.
Other trail users: Hikers only.

Land status: Wind Cave National Park.
Fees and permits: N/A
Maps: National Geographic/Trails Illustrated topo map No. 238; free Park Service map and brochure of Wind Cave National Park available at the visitor center.
Trail contact: Wind Cave National Park, RR 1, Box 190, Hot Springs, SD 57747; (605) 745-4600; www.nps.gov/wica.

Hiking Wind Cave National Park provides rare opportunities for solitude and glimpses of our vanishing American prairie.

Finding the trailhead: To access the trailhead from the visitor center, drive north for 1.75 miles on U.S. Highway 385 until it intersects with SD 87. Continue 0.62 mile farther along SD 87 to the Lookout Point/Centennial Trail trailhead, which is marked distinctly.

The Hike

Few trails in the Black Hills offer the opportunity to view both a pristine prairie and a riparian ecosystem. The trail is easy with only a few ascents and descents, but some hikers may at times categorize the trail as moderate because of the eight stream crossings, five of which must sometimes be made without the help of logs. Park rangers have placed flattened logs over several of the streams to facilitate crossings. If you do not wish to embark on the entire loop trip, turn back at the end of the Lookout Point Trail, which is 1.9 miles one-way.

The trail begins by gently rising onto a tallgrass prairie ecosystem, characterized by a variety of grasses. In summer the prairie may show a beautiful progression of wildflowers. After 1 mile of easy walking, the trail reaches its zenith at Lookout Point, elevation 4,480 feet. The trail does not lead directly to Lookout Point, but that is just a short jaunt to your right. From there you'll see views of the 1997 prescribed fire.

From here the trail gently descends and cuts through the northern end of Prairie Dog Canyon. Abundant evidence demonstrates just how these small rodents, acting in concert, can drastically alter the prairie to meet their own requirements. Because prairie dogs must rely for survival on defensive strategies, they have cut the grass to improve their vistas. The changes attract other wildlife species such as bison, coyotes, and rattlesnakes. Be forewarned! One park naturalist who frequently hikes Wind Cave trails says that he must invariably modify his route to avoid a dangerously close approach with bison.

At a trail juncture with the Highland Creek Trail 0.9 mile later (this trail comes in from the south, or your right), you should stay left or backtrack on the Lookout Point trail. If you elect to complete the loop, 2.1 miles of walking remain. From the junction the trail descends 200 feet to Beaver Creek. As it does, the vegetation changes abruptly to ponderosa pine, the invader. If not checked, ponderosa would soon encroach beyond its historic boundaries and take over much of the prairie here. Prescribed burning conducted in the spring and fall curtails its growth.

From Beaver Creek proceed west. About 0.2 mile later, just before it joins the Centennial Trail (which you'll take to the west, or your left), the trail crosses the creek and then does so again on four different occasions. Dry-footed crossings may require imagination and enterprise, particularly following heavy rains.

The hike along Beaver Creek offers views of variegated rock bluffs, some a brilliant orange. High caves cut into the bluffs, and trees that have somehow established a toehold stand as sentinels at the entrances to some of these high rock cuts. Along the stream proper, footprints of hikers mingle with those of bison and deer, and it is not uncommon to see either.

As the trail nears its end, waters from Cold Spring Creek merge with those of Beaver Creek, which continues its eastern trend. Near the terminus the trail ascends and shortly concludes at the Lookout Point/Centennial trailhead.

Miles and Directions

0.0 Start at the Lookout Point/Centennial trailhead on SD 87.

1.0 The trail reaches its highest elevation at Lookout Point.

2.0 At the Lookout Point/Highland Creek Trail junction, stay northeast (left) on Lookout Point Trail.

2.3 At the junction with Centennial Trail, turn west (to the left) onto the Centennial Trail.

4.0 The end of the loop at the Lookout Point/Centennial trailhead.

44 Sanctuary-Centennial-Highland Creek Trail

A one-way route linking several trails in Wind Cave National Park, allowing hikers to experience a variety of park habitats. You might consider arranging for a shuttle back to the starting point.

See map on page 134
Start: At the Sanctuary trailhead on South Dakota Highway 87, about 6.5 miles north of the visitor center.
Distance: About 9 miles one-way.
Approximate hiking time: A full day.
Difficulty: Moderately strenuous.
Seasons: Best from spring through fall.
Other trail users: Hikers only.

Land status: Wind Cave National Park.
Fees and permits: N/A
Maps: National Geographic/Trails Illustrated topo map No. 238; free Park Service map and brochure of Wind Cave National Park available at the visitor center.
Trail contact: Wind Cave National Park, RR 1, Box 190, Hot Springs, SD 57747; (605) 745-4600; www.nps.gov/wica.

Finding the trailhead: Take U.S. Highway 385 north from the visitor center for 1.5 miles, then take SD 87 north for about 5 miles to the Sanctuary trailhead, on the right.

The Hike

The Sanctuary Trail's northern terminus is located where two ecosystems meet: the prairie grassland and the ponderosa pine. So much of the suggested 9-mile route weaves in and out of such "edge" conditions that the possibilities of seeing wildlife are excellent. Start early to enhance your chances and, more important, to avoid the summer heat.

Within 0.75 mile after departing, the trail ascends slightly and passes over a small saddle. The trail then descends and enters a grassland community in a narrow valley. Periodically, you'll see views of Lookout Tower on Rankin Ridge. From here the trail cuts up to avoid the wet bottom and continues, though at times indistinctly, to its junction with the Centennial Trail.

Just prior to the link, the Sanctuary Trail passes by what appear to be the remnants of an old homestead. All that remains is a rock foundation measuring about 16 by 20 feet and another much smaller rock formation that perhaps formed an old root cellar. Nearby is a small stream.

The prairie here contains a rich assortment of flora and fauna, and it is appropriate that this area can be approached from several different routes and by several different trails. About 2 miles from the trailhead, the Centennial and Sanctuary Trails cross, and it is at this point that hikers should follow the Centennial Trail, which is easier and more consistently marked.

The Centennial Trail portion of this route proceeds through a series of small rises, passing through a ponderosa forest spotted with pockets of grassland. Bison wallows are numerous. The route approaches its first steep descent 3.5 miles from the Sanctuary trailhead, and it is here that the hike might be categorized as mildly strenuous, primarily because of the slope. The trail descends from 4,200 feet to 4,020 feet, at which point hikers approach Beaver Creek and a milepost marker.

Turn left and follow a short section of Centennial Trail for 0.25 mile until it intersects with the Highland Creek Trail. In times of high water, the trail crosses a "very wet" Beaver Creek three times before it intersects with the Highland Creek Trail. The Highland Creek Trail, which begins 4 miles to the north along Park Road 5, climbs in a southwesterly direction almost as quickly as the Centennial Trail dropped. The trail forms a junction with the Lookout Point Trail 0.5 mile later.

Continue following the Highland Creek Trail as it progresses south, then southeast, then south once again through another grassland community. Because you can frequently see US 385, there is little danger of getting lost. Nevertheless, you may sometimes have difficulty remaining on the Highland Creek Trail since it is interlaced with bison trails, which are often more distinct (and hence confusing) than the park trail. If you lose the trail, search for markers by using your binoculars and sweeping right or left. Don't dismay: Markers do exist, unless they have been knocked down by bison, which use the markers for scratching posts and in their agony (or ecstasy) sometimes uproot the posts creating difficulty for the park's trail-maintenance program. Because of heavy bison activity in the area, 1.5 miles south of the point where the Highland Creek Trail joins the Lookout Point Trail, some markers may lean and dip into the prairie grass.

About 2.5 miles from the intersection of the Centennial and the Highland Creek Trails, the path reenters a thin stand of ponderosa pine, then drops 300 feet (from 4,200 to 3,900 feet) where, at 2.8 miles after the junction, it intersects with the Wind Cave Canyon Trail. This latter trail is flanked by canyon walls containing a variety of bird nests. You'll see cliff swallows and perhaps great horned owls. Look for woodpeckers in the standing dead trees.

The East Bison Flats Trail junction is reached 0.5 mile later. Continue on the Wind Cave Canyon Trail for 0.5 mile, passing near the park's sewage treatment center to the trail's end across from the visitor center on US 385. You'll have to find a ride to get back to your starting point. Rides from fellow campers seem easy to obtain. Another suggestion, however, is to shuttle vehicles before departing rather than having someone wait at trail's end.

Miles and Directions

0.0 Start at the Sanctuary trailhead.

0.75 Ascend a small saddle.

1.5 Take the Centennial Trail south at the junction, staying straight.

4.0 At the T, take the Centennial Trail east (left) for 0.25 mile.

4.5 Follow the Highland Creek Trail to the right (south) at the junction.

5.0   At the junction with Lookout Point Trail, turn left (south) onto Highland Creek.

8.0   Follow the Wind Cave Canyon Trail to the right (northwest direction) at the junction.

8.5   East Bison Flats Trail comes in from the south. Do not take it. Continue straight.

9.0   This is the end of Wind Cave Canyon Trail. The visitor center is across the road.

45 Highland Creek-Centennial Loop

A loop hike that combines two trails through an area of immense, diverse beauty.

See map on page 134
Start: From the Highland Creek trailhead on NPS Road 5, 2.8 miles east of South Dakota Highway 87.
Distance: 7-mile loop.
Approximate hiking time: Plan on most of a day.
Difficulty: Easy to moderately strenuous.
Other trail users: Hikers only.

Seasons: Best from spring through fall.
Fees and permits: N/A
Land status: Wind Cave National Park.
Maps: National Geographic/Trails Illustrated topo map No. 238.
Trail contact: Wind Cave National Park, RR 1, Box 190, Hot Springs, SD 57747; (605) 745-4600; www.nps.gov/wica.

Finding the trailhead: Take U.S. Highway 385 north from the Wind Cave National Park Visitor Center for 0.5 mile, then follow SD 87 north for 7 miles to an NPS 5 road sign on the right. The Centennial Trail trailhead is 1.25 miles in on the right. The Highland Creek trailhead is 1 mile farther, also on the right.

We suggest leaving your vehicle at the Highland Creek parking lot and beginning the loop hike there. The trail concludes at the Centennial trailhead, from where you must walk an additional 1 mile back to the vehicle.

The Hike

This loop option is a relatively flat, natural-history trail, meandering through the tallgrass prairie. Throughout, the trail offers scenic vistas of the Black Hills. The final miles pass over a forest trail.

The hike begins on a tallgrass prairie plateau that offers panoramic views. As the trail proceeds counterclockwise, it parallels Rankin Ridge and is separated by about a mile from the Red Valley to the east. In places the trail is faint and markers are sometimes infrequent. Be sure your travels proceed in a southeasterly direction. Sharp-tailed grouse are abundant in the high grasslands, and more than one hiker has been unnerved by the flurry of wings that suddenly erupts as feet and bird almost collide.

As the trail descends 0.75 mile from the trailhead, you will find yourself suddenly in the midst of a huge prairie-dog town where incessant chirping fills the air. Often the chirps serve not to warn of hikers but rather of a fat coyote or two lurking near the town's edge. To facilitate defensive vision, prairie dogs have chopped down the grasses. Their efforts help to delineate trail markers, obscured elsewhere by grass. Note also the huge ant mounds throughout.

Upon leaving the prairie-dog town, the trail may again be indistinct. Refer to your topo map and compass and notice that the trail now veers slightly southwest (to your right) and parallels a small stand of ponderosa pine. The next trail marker is 0.25 mile away on top of a hill. Stay straight at this point, keeping the pines on your left. As you ascend the next plateau, Rankin Ridge Fire Tower is clearly visible straight in front of you (2 to 2.5 miles away).

The route now heads south. Although game trails might entice you toward the woods, remain on the small ridge. Trail markers will soon lead you to this trail's intersection with the Sanctuary Trail. Take this trail to the right then remain on Sanctuary, which proceeds northwest for about 1 mile until it intersects with the Centennial Trail. Bison wallows and muddy water holes are numerous, as are bison. Here hikers enter a beautiful broad valley. Take time to sit quietly and observe another prairie-dog town that, like the others, is often frequented by bison, antelope, deer, and coyotes.

The trail drops to the valley floor where it intersects with the Centennial Trail. Follow this to the right, in a northeasterly direction, where it enters a forest. The remaining 1.25 miles are well marked. About 0.25 mile from the terminus, look for a prescribed burn. At trail's end, continue walking 1 mile to retrieve the vehicle.

Miles and Directions

0.0 Start at the Highland Creek Trailhead, going south.

0.75 Arrive at a prairie-dog town; be alert for snakes.

1.0 There's a trail marker on top of the hill.

3.0 Follow the Sanctuary Trail northwest (to the right) at the junction.

4.5 Follow the Centennial Trail to the northeast (right) at the junction.

6.0 Reach the Centennial Trail Trailhead and dirt road.

7.0 This is the end of 1-mile walk to the east (to vehicle) and the Highland Creek Trailhead.

46 Boland Ridge Trail

A one-way trek over Boland Ridge, terminating at the park boundary fence.

See map on page 134
Start: At the Boland Ridge Trailhead.
Distance: 2.7 miles out and back.
Approximate hiking time: 2 to 4 hours.

Difficulty: Moderately strenuous.
Other trail users: Hikers only.
Seasons: Best from spring through fall.
Land status: Wind Cave National Park.

Fees and permits: N/A
Maps: National Geographic/Trails Illustrated topo map No. 238; free Park Service map and brochure of Wind Cave National Park available at the visitor center.

Trail contact: Wind Cave National Park, RR 1, Box 190, Hot Springs, SD 57747; (605) 745-4600; www.nps.gov/wica.

Finding the trailhead: Take U.S. Highway 385 north from the Wind Cave National Park Visitor Center for 0.5 mile, then follow South Dakota Highway 87 north for 7 miles to the NPS 5 road sign on the right. Proceed on Park Road 5 for 6.4 miles, taking the first dirt road on the left (NPS 6). Go 0.8 mile to the trailhead, on the right.

The Hike

The trail mostly traverses gullies and the ridges of Boland Ridge in the Red Valley. Wonderful vistas are offered of the valley, the prairies, and, on clear days, Badlands National Park.

This moderately strenuous hike begins by following a faint dirt road in the tall-grass prairie. In 0.1 mile hikers cross a tiny creek, which might be dry in times of drought. On our late-July hike, the creek was narrow but flowing freely. Whether or not the creek is present depends on capricious weather patterns.

After crossing a meadow, ascend the first ridge of Boland, still on the old, unused road. The trail is well marked, but the markers are only 2 feet high and are often difficult to see in the high grass. The trail follows an easterly and slightly northeast direction and soon encounters another meadow, alive in summer with vibrant wildflowers. Continue along a series of rolling ups and downs as the trail bisects Boland Ridge. Each ascent offers a different perspective. After the last major descent and about 0.5 mile of hiking, the trail terminates at the park's boundary fence. Now you must retrace your steps.

This area is prime bison habitat (as we discovered that day) and the many gullies easily hide the huge beasts. At times they seem to appear out of nowhere like huge dark shadows. On the day we were there, the majority of the Wind Cave herd had migrated to this area and was in the midst of the age-old annual mating cycle. The noise alone was alarming and could be heard a mile away, sometimes carrying a sound reminiscent of a lion's unthrottled roar. We felt as though we were among the chosen few, watching as we were the herd's behavior for more than an hour. An unexpected prairie hailstorm broke our observation and sent us scurrying for shelter. It also stampeded the herd.

Many trails such as this one in Wind Cave are easily bushwhacked. From Boland Ridge Trail, roads are visible from the ridges and one could hike along the top of Boland Ridge. As always, carry water, a topo map, and a compass to enhance hiking pleasure, comfort, and safety.

47 Rankin Ridge Nature Trail

A short interpretive loop trail that ascends through ponderosa-pine forest, providing vistas of Wind Cave National Park and its immense surroundings.

See map on page 134
Start: From the Rankin Ridge parking lot at the fire tower off South Dakota Highway 87.
Distance: 1-mile loop.
Approximate hiking time: 1 hour.
Difficulty: Moderate.
Highest Elevation: 5,013 ft.
Seasons: Best from spring through fall.

Other trail users: Hikers only.
Land status: Wind Cave National Park.
Fees and permits: N/A
Maps: An interpretive brochure is available at the park's visitor center or at the trailhead.
Trail contact: Wind Cave National Park, RR 1, Box 190, Hot Springs, SD 57747; (605) 745-4600; www.nps.gov/wica.

Finding the trailhead: Take U.S. Highway 385 north from the park's visitor center to SD 87. Take SD 87 north for about 4 miles to the sign and the road for the fire tower, which is on the right. The Rankin Ridge trailhead is located in the fire tower's parking lot.

The Hike

This short trail provides a delightful climb up Rankin Ridge to sweeping views of the park and beyond. From the ridge the view suggests immense geological phenomena to the east. Red Valley cuts a spectacular swath through the foreground, while the Hog Back Ridge, with Bison Gap, suggests a ring engulfing the Black Hills. The White River Badlands, once a part of the Black Hills, shimmer in the distance. The trail is well interpreted and the park provides a booklet (available at the trailhead and visitor center) for the fourteen interpreted stops.

Following the park's suggested route, the trail begins on a northerly aspect. The trail ascends quickly, entering an area that is a prime example of a previous prescribed burning of ponderosa pines. Along the way, several log benches provide opportunities to rest and further explore the panorama sweeping before you. Bring your binoculars.

Approximately 0.5 mile from the trailhead, hikers reach the fire tower, at an elevation of 5,013 feet. Seventy-two steps climb to the tower's observation deck. Look west toward the heart of the Black Hills; the ancient updoming effect is apparent. A 0.5-mile descent on a dirt road passes through a ponderosa-pine forest and returns you to the parking lot.

48 Elk Mountain Nature Trail

A fun, informative loop hike suitable for the entire family.

See map on page 134
Start: At the Elk Mountain Campground, 1.24 miles northwest of the visitor center.
Distance: 1.2-mile loop.
Approximate hiking time: 1 to 1½ hours.
Difficulty: Easy.
Seasons: Best from spring through fall.
Other trail users: Hikers only.

Land status: Wind Cave National Park.
Fees and permits: N/A
Maps: An interpretive booklet is available at the trailhead or from the park visitor center.
Trail contact: Wind Cave National Park, RR1, Box 190, Hot Springs, SD 57747; (605) 745-4600; www.nps.gov/wica.

Finding the trailhead: The trail is readily accessible and is located at Elk Mountain Campground (the only designated campground in Wind Cave National Park), which is 1.24 miles northwest of the park's visitor center on U.S. Highway 385. The trailhead is opposite the campground's outdoor amphitheater.

The Hike

Following the path clockwise, it winds slightly upwards through a prairie environment. It then enters the ponderosa-pine forest, where remains of a 1991 wildfire linger. The interpretive booklet greatly enhances the walk, which has nine interpretive stops.

Badlands National Park

T he Lakota people call the Badlands Mako Sica, which means "land that is bad." The French trappers who traveled the region in the early 1800s arrived at a similar designation, calling them the *mauvaises terres a traverser,* or "bad lands to travel across." Badlands geology begins with the encroachment of oceans millions of years ago. Over the eons, these waters deposited many sediments. There followed a series of volcanic activities that contributed to the doming up of the Black Hills and, of course, the badlands deposits.

With the doming, rivers and streams began to flow from the evolving mountains, carrying with them some of the sediments deposited by ancient seas. Eventually these sandstones, banded clays, and limestones were redeposited in what came to be known as the White River Badlands, named for one of the rivers that transported a portion of these materials. Erosional forces then acted on these malleable sediments, creating some of the nation's most spectacular formations.

Today the landscape assumes many forms, all of which are related to the hardness of the sedimentary deposits and to the manner in which wind, rain, snow, and ice act on them. Only the most hardened sandstones remain, in a variety of shapes. Some appear as great castles and pyramids, others as fluted spires and mushroom-shaped rocks. When explorers, scientists, visitors, and hikers walked the land, they found these bizarre shapes fantastic as time added more dimension to them.

Here, too, were the fossilized remains of three-toed horses, prehistoric rhinos and pigs, saber-toothed cats, and an abundance of sea life. Today the 244,300 acres of the White River Badlands serve as a hiker's paradise, since the formations, with their spires and gullies, invite exploration. You'll be seeing the largest protected mixed-grass prairie in the United States, with 64,000 acres of wilderness. The Park Service maintains eight short trails in the badlands. In addition, adventurous souls have the opportunity to hike more freely in the backcountry (though it's more ecologically considerate to stick to paths created by humans or buffalo). The wilderness areas are discussed later in this section.

The shorter, marked trails in Badlands National Park offer opportunities to experience most of the park's geological oddities. With the exception of the Saddle Pass

A bison skull placed along a Badlands trail symbolizes the buffalo culture, which the government tried to eradicate. Sioux Chief Spotted Elk, maybe better known as Bigfoot, the name government soldiers called him, rode these rough, arid trails just prior to his rendezvous with fate December 1890 at nearby Wounded Knee.

Trail, these are relatively easy and have no significant elevation gain. Combined, these trails require several hours of hiking time, and opportunities abound to study nature and conduct photographic explorations. The Badlands Natural History Association has compiled interpretive booklets for three of the maintained trails: the Fossil Exhibit Trail, the Cliff Shelf Nature Trail, and the Door Trail. Purchase of these inexpensive guides is recommended for those who want to enhance their understanding of badlands topography. None of these trails ascends—or descends—more than a few hundred feet, so details on elevations are not included in this book.

When hiking, please remember the badlands terrain is very fragile. Exercise caution and try to minimize damage by remaining on established paths. Maintain a wary eye for bison and snakes. And carry water, particularly in summer when hiking the longer trails. The Badlands contain no potable water; all must be carried in. Because summer temperatures can and often do exceed one hundred degrees, each person needs to carry about a gallon per day. For those contemplating extended

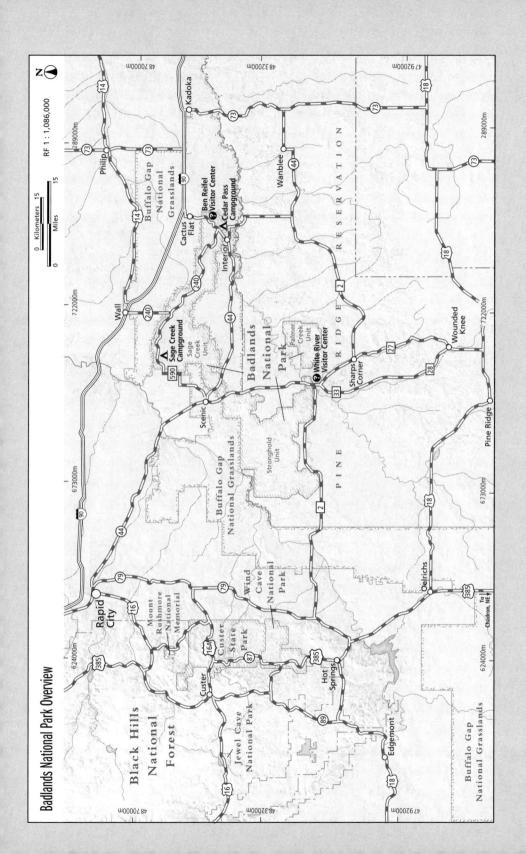

Badlands National Park Overview

trips, packing enough water presents the major obstacle. Open fires are not allowed anywhere in the park so carry a backpack stove. The park does not issue backcountry permits; nevertheless, hikers are advised to stop at the Ben Reifel Visitor Center for weather and wildlife information. Purchase a topo map and discuss trip plans with a ranger. Though park personnel do not mandate registration for wilderness hiking, they do recommend that hikers log their intentions.

Badlands National Park has an open policy for hikers, meaning that there are no closed areas with the exception of black-footed-ferret reintroduction sites. Mountain bikes and motorized vehicles are allowed on paved roads only; they are off-limits on all of the park's trails as well as throughout the various wilderness areas. Expect high winds and brief but violent thunderstorms year-round.

Badlands National Park is located in the southwestern part of South Dakota, about 70 miles east of the Black Hills of South Dakota. The Ben Reifel Visitor Center is located 83 miles east of Rapid City off Interstate 90 (exit 109) via the South Dakota State Highway 240 Loop road from Wall, or 72 miles east of Rapid City via South Dakota Highway 44. The park fee is $5.00 to $10.00 for one week's admission.

Another option is to continue east past Wall on I–90 to exit 131 (Cactus Flat). From there, take SD 240 south for 8.5 miles to the visitor center. For those coming from the south, go to the other visitor center, White River (open only in summer), which is on BIA Highway 27 about 8 miles north of Sharps Corner. The two campgrounds, Cedar Pass and Sage Creek Primitive Campground, are open all year on a first-come, first-served basis. Dogs are not allowed on the trails.

49 Castle Trail

A prairie hike flanking the beautiful formations along the Badlands Wall.

Start: At the Castle Trail trailhead across from the Door, Window, and Notch Trails on South Dakota Highway 240 (Badlands Loop Road).
Distance: 5 miles one-way.
Approximate hiking time: 4 to 6 hours.
Difficulty: Easy.
Seasons: Best late spring through fall.
Land status: Badlands National Park.
Fees and permits: Park fee.

Maps: National Geographic/Trails Illustrated Topo Map No. 239, 1:55,000 scale; Department of the Interior Geological Survey topographic map (metric) 43101-F8-PM-050; a free official map and guide pamphlet and interpretive booklets are available at the visitor centers.
Trail contact: Badlands National Park, P.O. Box 6, Interior, SD 57750-0006; (605) 433–5361; www.badlands.national-park.com.

Finding the trailhead: Take the Badlands Loop Road northeast from the Ben Reifel Visitor Center for approximately 2 miles to the trailhead at the eastern end of the Castle Trail, located across the road from the Door, Window, and Notch Trails. Access to portions of the trail is also

The sky is huge along the Castle Trail.

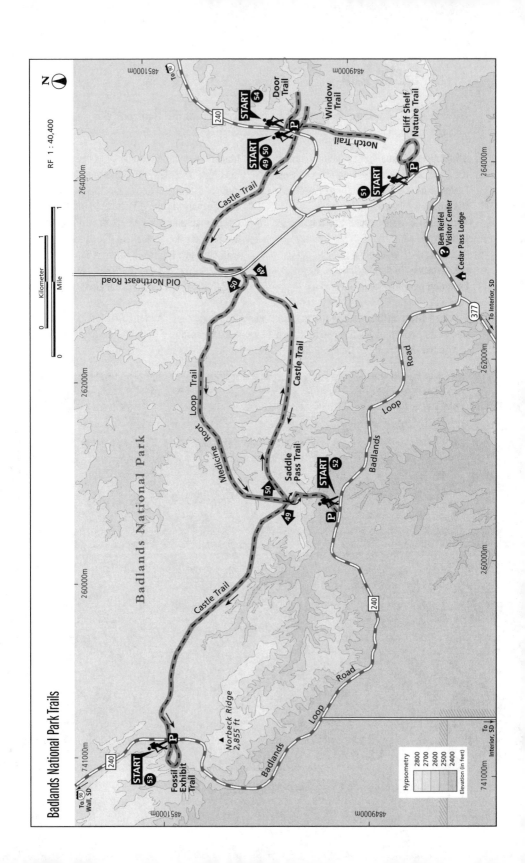

Badlands National Park Trails

RF 1 : 40,400

N

Kilometer

Mile

Badlands National Park

To 90
Wall, SD

240

Castle Trail

Norbeck Ridge
2,855 ft

Fossil Exhibit Trail

START 53

P

Medicine Root Loop Trail

Castle Trail

49

50

Saddle Pass Trail

START 52

P

49

50

Old Northeast Road

Castle Trail

START 49 50

START 54

Door Trail

P

Window Trail

Notch Trail

Cliff Shelf Nature Trail

START 51

P

Ben Reifel Visitor Center

Cedar Pass Lodge

Badlands Loop Road

Badlands Loop Road

240

377

To Interior, SD

To Interior, SD

Hypsometry
2800
2700
2600
2500
2400
Elevation (in feet)

available from the top of the Saddle Pass Trail, about 1.5 miles northwest of the Ben Reifel Visitor Center along the Loop Road. The western terminus of the trail is 5 miles west of the visitor center on SD 240, across the road from the Fossil Exhibit Trail.

The Hike

From the Door and Window Trail access, the Castle Trail begins at an elevation of 2,664 feet and progresses through a native mixed-grass prairie while flanking a badlands formation known as the Wall. Castle Trail is the longest of the park's marked trails and is not heavily traveled. After 1 mile the trail crosses the Old Northeast Road and continues its generally westward course, passing through an assortment of formations that provide mute testimony that the trail deserves the name ascribed to it by the National Park Service.

The trail ends across the road from the Fossil Exhibit Trail, 5 miles west of the visitor center, though there is another possibility. You can make a 4-mile loop by hiking west on the Castle Trail for 1 mile and then taking the Medicine Root Loop Trail west, accessed from the Old Northeast Road. The main trail continues for about 1 mile then loops back east on the Castle Trail for another 2 miles, at which point it returns you to your vehicle. This same type of combination is possible from the west end of the trail.

Miles and Directions

0.0 Start at the eastern Castle Trail trailhead.

1.0 Cross the Old Northeast Road.

2.0 Continue straight through intersection with Medicine Root Loop Trail.

5.0 The trail ends across the road from the Fossil Exhibit Trail.

50 Medicine Root Loop

A hike that offers a connecting loop within the Castle Trail.

See map on page 152

Start: At the Castle Trail trailhead across from the Door, Window, and Notch Trails on South Dakota Highway 240 (Badlands Loop Road).

Distance: 5-mile lollipop.

Approximate hiking time: 3 to 5 hours.

Difficulty: Easy.

Seasons: Best from spring through fall.

Land status: Badlands National Park.

Fees and permits: Park fee.

Maps: National Geographic/Trails Illustrated Topo Map No. 239, 1:55,000 scale; Department of the Interior Geological Survey topographic map (metric) 43101-F8-PM-050; free official map and guide pamphlet and interpretive booklets are available at the visitor centers.

Trail contact: Badlands National Park, P.O. Box 6, Interior, SD 57750-0006; (605) 433-5361; www.badlands.national-park.com.

Finding the trailhead: Take the SD 240 Loop Road northeast from the Ben Reifel Visitor Center for approximately 2 miles to the trail's parking area on the right. The trailhead is located across the road from the Door, Window, and Notch Trails.

Medicine Root Loop can be accessed from either end of the Castle Trail, or from the Saddle Pass Trail, which is 2 miles west of the Ben Reifel Visitor Center.

The Hike

The Medicine Root Loop Trail is a flat, easy walk along a narrow dirt path through the grassland area just north of the Castle Trail. As one walks along this plateau, grasslands sweep to the north while the jagged Wall formations rise to the south. Other formations range from short, flat, sod-covered "tables" to lofty spires. The area surrounding the trail is covered with cactus. Grasses hide desert wildflowers. Metal posts are abundant and serve to distinguish the trail from game paths. Medicine Root derives its name from the numerous plants that were once used here by Native Americans. Photo opportunities abound throughout. Medicine Root ends at the junction of Saddle Pass and Castle Trail.

To complete the loop, take the Castle Trail (marked by signs) leading east. From this point the trail ambles along the base of the rock formations. The level trail is somewhat rocky but soon becomes a narrow dirt path.

51 Cliff Shelf Nature Trail

An interpretive trail along an ancient cliff shelf that collapsed long ago from the imposing cliffs above.

See map on page 152
Start: From the Cliff Shelf trailhead 0.5 mile east of the Ben Reifel Visitor Center.
Distance: 0.5-mile loop.
Approximate hiking time: 30 minutes.
Difficulty: Moderate.
Seasons: Best from spring through fall.

Land status: Badlands National Park.
Fees and permits: Park fee.
Maps: Trail booklets may be purchased at the Ben Reifel Visitor Center or the trailhead box.
Trail contact: Badlands National Park, P.O. Box 6, Interior, SD 57750-0006; (605) 433-5361; www.badlands.national-park.com.

Finding the trailhead: The Cliff Shelf Nature Trail can be accessed from a point 0.5 mile east of the Ben Reifel Visitor Center on the Badlands Loop Road (South Dakota Highway 240). The parking lot is small and not suitable for cars towing trailers.

The Hike

Fascinating natural-history stories exist here at the collapsed Cliff Shelf, which fell years ago due to underground moisture. The facts of the area are thoroughly interpreted in materials created by the Badlands Natural History Association.

The trail undulates up and down through a wooded prairie, but is wide and has a stairway. A portion of the trail is barrier-free and thus wheelchair accessible. The park has provided a rest bench midway through the walk. You'll be treated to wonderful views of the White River Valley.

52 Saddle Pass Trail

A short and steep trail through a pass, following a path once used by early travelers. The Saddle Pass is impassable right after rains and still slippery when at all wet.

See map on page 152
Start: At the trailhead on the Badlands Loop Road (South Dakota Highway 240), 2 miles west of the Ben Reifel Visitor Center.
Distance: 0.6 mile out and back.
Approximate hiking time: 45 minutes.
Difficulty: Strenuous.
Seasons: Best from spring through fall.
Land status: Badlands National Park.
Fees and permits: Park fee.

Maps: National Geographic/Trails Illustrated Topo Map No. 239, 1:55,000 scale; Department of the Interior Geological Survey topographic map (metric) 43101-F8-PM-050; free official map and guide pamphlet and interpretive booklets are available at the visitor centers.
Trail contact: Badlands National Park, P.O. Box 6, Interior, SD 57750-0006; (605) 433-5361; www.badlands.national-park.com.

Finding the trailhead: The Saddle Pass Trail can be accessed from the Badlands Loop Road (SD 240), about 2 miles west of the Ben Reifel Visitor Center.

The Hike

The trail begins with an upward scramble through rocks. Simultaneously the trail provides grand vistas of the park, particularly at the summit. At times, especially when wet, the trail can be treacherous—the clay soil turns to "gumbo," which is very slippery and sticky. The trail's dry, loose stones can sometimes act like ball bearings.

At the summit the Saddle Pass Trail links with both the Castle Trail and the Medicine Root Loop Trail. From here, hikers have a choice of descending on the route they traveled upward or linking with one of these two trails.

In the early days, travelers from the north proceeding south to the town of Interior would leave their buggies at the top of the trail. They would then attempt to coax horses down the steep track. If the horses balked, riders left them here with the buggies, retrieving them upon their return from Interior—a 6-mile trek each way.

53 Fossil Exhibit Trail

A short, barrier-free loop to an exhibit of area fossils.

See map on page 152
Start: At the trailhead, 5 miles northwest of the Ben Reifel Visitor Center.
Distance: 0.25-mile loop.
Approximate hiking time: ½ hour.
Difficulty: Extremely easy.
Seasons: Spring through fall.

Land status: Badlands National Park.
Fees and permits: Park fee.
Maps: A self-guiding booklet is available at the trail kiosk or visitor center.
Trail contact: Badlands National Park, P.O. Box 6, Interior, SD 57750-0006; (605) 433-5361; www.badlands.national-park.com.

Finding the trailhead: The Fossil Exhibit Trail is located 5 miles west of the Ben Reifel Visitor Center on the Badlands Loop Road (South Dakota Highway 240).

The Hike

At the Fossil Exhibit, Badlands National Park has created replicas of fossils indigenous to the Badlands, and they are exhibited along this trail in glass-covered bins. The trail is wheelchair accessible. If you are here in the summer, attend a talk given by a park naturalist about the fossil history of the park.

54 The Door, Window, and Notch Trails

Easy journeys to view some of the park's most rugged rock formations.

See map on page 152
Start: All three trails are accessed from a parking lot on Badlands Loop Road, 2 miles east of the Ben Reifel Visitor Center.
Distance: The Door Trail, 0.75 mile out and back; the Window Trail is 0.25 mile total; the Notch Trail is 1.5 miles out and back.
Difficulty: Moderate for Door; easy for the Window Trail; moderate for Notch Trail.

Seasons: Best from spring through fall.
Land status: Badlands National Park.
Fees and permits: Park fee.
Maps: N/A; small brown posts assist you on the Door and Notch Trails.
Trail contact: Badlands National Park, P.O. Box 6, Interior, SD 57750-0006; (605) 433-5361; www.badlands.national-park.com.

Finding the trailhead: The trails are accessible from a parking lot 2 miles east of the Ben Reifel Visitor Center, along Badlands Loop Road 240.

Views from on top make it worthwhile to climb the ladder on the Notch Trail.

The Hike

The first 100 yards of the **Door Trail** are barrier-free and allow even visitors in wheelchairs to enter and pass through the "door," where some of the Badlands' most rugged terrain greets you. The rest of the trail is rough but flat, and sturdy shoes are recommended. If one goes off-trail, the terrain is fragile and many edges are loose. Exercise caution!

Throughout the area hikers are treated to vast panoramas of spires, "doors in the walls," and steep gullies. Because of the interplay of light, the design changes constantly—almost whimsically—creating a photographer's paradise, especially in the morning and early evening. Nothing here is ever the same.

The **Window Trail** is an easy walk to a natural "window" in the Badlands Wall, through which visitors can peek at a stupendous view of the eroded canyon. The trail is also barrier-free, though trail conditions can be rough.

The Notch Trail is a hike of great beauty but one not recommended to those with a fear of heights. For the first 0.25 mile, it meanders through the canyon floor around rocks and delicate prairie flowers. Then it reaches a sixty-one-rung ladder, which is cabled into the hill. Here's where those afraid of heights might want to turn back.

Upon reaching the top of the ladder, hikers follow the scuffed trail that winds around rock ledges above the canyon for about 0.5 mile until it emerges and ends at the top of a cliff, providing a commanding overlook of the valley. Here, you stand on part of a cliff that collapsed long ago and formed the Cliff Shelf Nature Trail, lying directly below. Use caution, as this trail can be slippery when wet. Brown posts mark the route. Retrace your steps, descending the ladder this time, to return to the trailhead.

Additional Hikes

For those interested in exploring the Badlands wilderness, the park offers several options that provide liberal access. Badlands National Park encompasses the nation's largest prairie wilderness, which hikers may roam at will. Leave the road behind and explore the Sage Creek Wilderness Area, which extends over 64,144 acres, or trek the Stronghold and Palmer Creek Units in the Pine Ridge Indian Reservation, though still managed by the park.

Sage Creek Wilderness Area

From the Ben Reifel Visitor Center, take the Badlands Loop Road (South Dakota Highway 240) west for 24 miles to Sage Creek Rim Road, which comes in from the left. Follow this road for 5.9 miles to a turnout on the left. A camper registration box is located here and animal/people trails can be seen wandering into the wilderness area. No marked trails exist in the wilderness areas, but half the fun results from striking out on your own.

Another option is to follow the Sage Creek Rim Road for 11 miles to the Sage Creek Campground (32 miles from the Ben Reifel Visitor Center). Again, there are no designated trails from the campground; however, a multitude of animal/people paths strike out from here. Most of the trails soon give out and hikers are on their own to wander at will in solitude and the land's overwhelming beauty.

More than 500 bison call Sage Creek home. Use extreme caution around these large mammals, especially during the rut season (July through September). Do not approach within 200 yards.

About one-third of the Sage Creek Wilderness landscape consists of eroded and nearly barren badlands. The remainder of the park consists of a mixed-grass prairie ecosystem. Though hikers may see wildlife in most Badlands areas, the park's remote wilderness tends to attract the largest wildlife concentrations. Look for coyotes, prairie dogs, sharp-tailed grouse, wild turkeys, eagles, rabbits, and hawks as well as for the bison, pronghorn, mule deer, and even bighorn sheep.

Stronghold and Palmer Creek Units

The Stronghold and Palmer Creek areas are within the Pine Ridge Reservation in the southwestern part of Badlands National Park. The White River Visitor Center is located between the two. Potential users should first inquire at the visitor center to determine prevailing conditions, particularly for the more remote Stronghold Unit. Visitors must cross private land for most access; please be very respectful of private property.

To reach this area, proceed southwest from the Ben Reifel Visitor Center for 2.5 miles to the town of Interior. Take South Dakota Highway 44 west for 39 miles to the town of Scenic. From Scenic, follow Forest Roads 589 and 27 south for 20 miles to the White River Visitor Center. Or, from the Wounded Knee site in southwestern South Dakota, take FR 27 north. The White River Visitor Center is 8 miles north of Sharps Corner.

The wilderness areas of Badlands National Park are intriguing because of the freedom they offer. Hikers can strike off in any direction. Wander through bluffs and prairie grass, or follow dry streambeds. In these areas, hikers can find solitude, peace, and a stark beauty found nowhere else.

Backpackers venturing into the wilderness are free to roam at will, camping anywhere, providing they are at least 0.5 mile off the road and not visible to traffic. Park officials also ask you to remember that others will follow your example and that you should help preserve the land by practicing zero-impact camping. Do not disturb any fossils or artifacts you might find, but do report any finds to park rangers.

The Lakota people consider the Stronghold area sacred. Please do not touch any objects that they may have left behind.

The Long Trails

The Black Hills offer such incredible diversity of terrain for hikers that we've included two longer routes for those who cannot get enough of this wilderness.

The Centennial Trail opened in June 1989 to celebrate one hundred years of statehood for South Dakota. This 111-mile trail has a lofty beginning and magnificent ending. Proceeding from north to south, the trail begins at Bear Butte and Bear Butte Lake, where Crazy Horse presided over a Council of Nations that was determined to protect the Black Hills from outside encroachment. The trail ends in Wind Cave National Park, an area best known for its subterranean features but equally touted for its rolling prairie features that host many natural dramas that have their underpinnings in grass.

The second long trail is the George S. Mickelson Trail, South Dakota's first rails-to-trails project. It traces the historic Burlington Northern Railroad line over 114 miles from Deadwood to Edgemont. When the rail line was abandoned in 1983, local residents recognized the recreational potential of the land. Backed by then governor George S. Mickelson, the trail was named in his honor. Completed in the fall of 1998, the trail is open to those who travel on foot, on skis, on bicycle, or on horseback. From end to end it offers a panoramic view of the history and the natural splendor of the heart of the Black Hills.

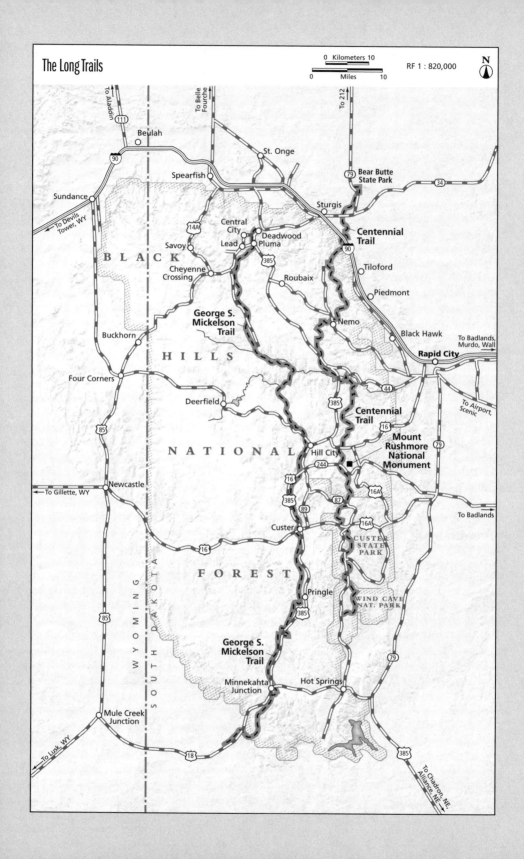

The Long Trails

Kilometers 10

Miles 10

RF 1 : 820,000

N

55 Centennial Trail

The land between Bear Butte and Wind Cave is inspiring. Here, the curtain goes up daily, for there are lakes, peaks, historic areas, and landscapes that teem with wildlife and provide hikers with endless variety. What all this boils down to is that the Centennial Trail does precisely what it was established to do: It provides users with an opportunity to relive the fabulous history that is South Dakota's and to evaluate for themselves what magnificent natural treasures the state still retains.

The Centennial Trail can be backpacked in one grand outing or can be hiked segmentally. Mountain bikes are permitted in most areas, except for the nationally designated wilderness areas, such as the Black Elk Wilderness Area in the Black Hills National Forest and in National Park Service–administered areas of Wind Cave and Mount Rushmore. For those planning an extended Centennial trek, about the only real concern is potable water. That problem can be solved by carrying a water-purification kit, such as a Katadyn water filter, capable of filtering out the cyst-causing *Giardia*.

Finding campsites is not a problem, since these can be fashioned nearly anywhere in the wilderness and primitive settings. Backpackers are encouraged to make primitive use of the land, using zero-impact camping methods. In Custer State Park camping is permitted only in the French Creek Natural Area. For all other areas, you must camp off the trail and essentially out of sight. You must use good camping hygiene as well.

The Centennial Trail is 111 miles long, and assuming the somewhat moderate pace of about 10 miles each day, the entire trail can be covered in ten to twelve days. Obviously backpackers will need to become students of lightweight food products or toss in the towel and rely on the lightweight foods offered by such companies as Mountain House, generally sold out of sporting-goods stores.

For those preferring to hike segmentally, the Centennial Trail provides twenty-two trailheads, conveniently located for excursions of 4 to 10 miles. Campsites often are located near the trailheads or along the route. If so, we have noted them.

The following provides a breakdown of trailheads and highlights the major features hikers will encounter between trailheads. For many, hiking the trail segmentally may well satisfy limitations imposed by time constraints. Trail users will be delighted to learn that with but few exceptions, the Centennial Trail is very well marked.

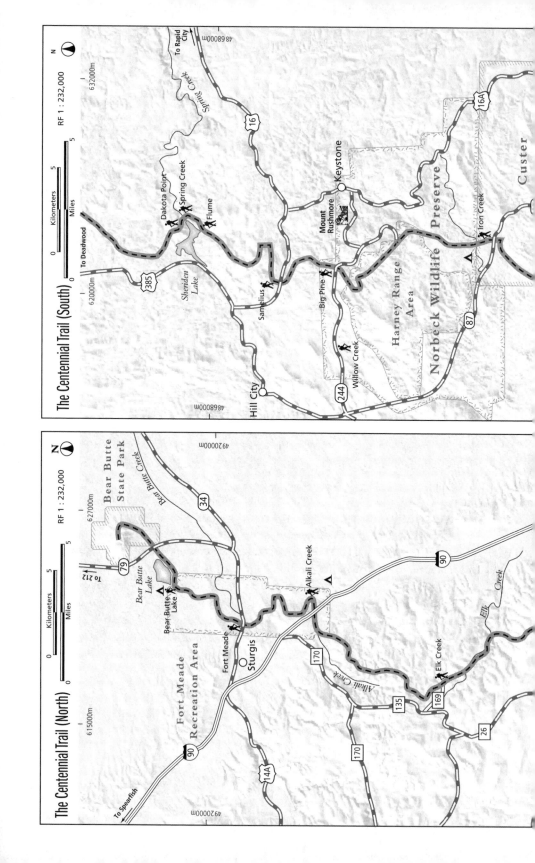

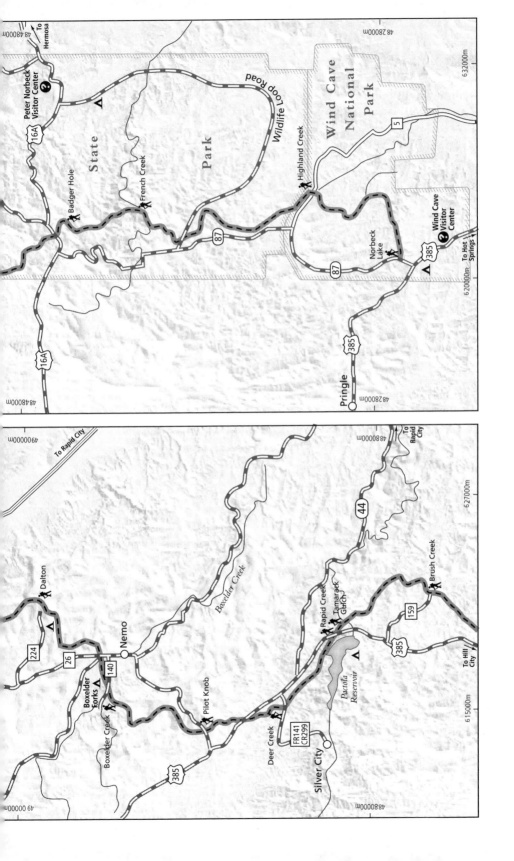

Trailheads (North to South)

Bear Butte Campground (Mile 0)

Starting from the crest of Bear Butte, the trail drops 4 miles, passing the Bear Butte Visitor Center and soon crossing South Dakota Highway 79, where it proceeds past Bear Butte Lake. From the lake, the trail courses across grasslands and enters, at mile 6, the Fort Meade Recreation Area. The prairie trail continues for another 2 miles, crossing South Dakota Highway 34 near Fort Meade Veterans Hospital.

For a fee, the state offers a campground on Bear Butte Lake. The campground is conveniently located and provides hikers with a jumping-off point as well as an ideal spot from which to view the myriad waterfowl. Alternately, at about mile 6, a primitive campsite could be fashioned near the crest just before the trail drops down to the more civilized surroundings of the Veterans Administration Center at Fort Meade, which offers no camping.

Fort Meade Trailhead (Mile 10.5)

Follow SD 34 east from Sturgis for 2 miles to the historic military post by the same name. From here, this short segment proceeds south and approaches the famous Fort Meade Cemetery.

Alkali Creek Trailhead (Mile 12.5)

From Sturgis follow Interstate 90 for 5 miles to the trailhead. From here, the trail proceeds south and parallels the general flow of Alkali Creek for about 5 miles, rising steeply as it progresses. The trail then proceeds in an up-and-down manner until its junction with the next trailhead.

Elk Creek Trailhead (Mile 23.5)

From Sturgis, drive south on I–90 then south on Forest Road 170 to Forest Road 135, then to Forest Road 168. From here the trail proceeds along a small creek, which in September is often dry, for almost 2 miles. It then ascends through stands of ponderosa pine that provide ideal elk habitat. Bands of elk wander here, and alert hikers see them often.

After ascending the ridge, the trail drops precipitously into the Elk Creek drainage, where a sign advises trail users that they must determine whether they wish to proceed along a primitive, unmaintained trail that parallels Elk Creek or follow the maintained horse trail. Whichever trail hikers select eventually routes users to the canyon edge, where it ascends very steeply for about 0.5 mile to a logging road. Pay close attention here, for Centennial Trail markers may be limited; a number of logging roads in this area resemble the trail and often create confusion and momentary panic. In one area, where the trail intersects with three logging roads all at the same spot, it can become darn confusing. Take time to search for the markers. If you follow a road for several hundred yards and don't see a Centennial Trail marker, assume you've made a wrong turn. Retrace your steps and look again. Markers do exist, though time may have dimmed them.

This section of the trail is 10.9 miles long. At 8.6 miles from this trailhead, the trail passes through a fence and enters a jeep road, which it follows for slightly more than a mile. The trail then becomes a traditional trail and remains as such until it concludes at Dalton trailhead.

Possible campsites are numerous, particularly in the Elk Creek drainage. There is also a campsite at Dalton Lake, where you can replenish your water supply.

Dalton Trailhead (Mile 32.4)
From Sturgis, access FR 170 and follow it 4 miles to its intersection with Forest Road 26. Follow FR 26 for 10 miles until it intersects with Forest Road 224. The trailhead is at the end of FR 224. This section of trail proceeds through dense stands of timber and is alive with populations of deer.

Boxelder Creek Trailhead (Mile 40.6)
The route is the same as to Dalton, but remain on FR 26 for 3.5 miles until the road intersects with Forest Road 140. Follow FR 140 to the end. Like the preceding section, this one also contains nice populations of deer.

Pilot Knob Trailhead (Mile 46.6)
This section of the Centennial Trail is most easily accessed from Hill City by following U.S. Highway 385 north past Sheridan Lake and Pactola Reservoir. From Pactola, proceed about 8 miles to Forest Road 208. Follow FR 208 for 0.5 mile to the trailhead.

Deer Creek Trailhead (Mile 49.8)
Take the same route as the preceding, except from Pactola Reservoir, proceed only 2 miles to Forest Road 141 (County Road 299).

Rapid Creek Trailhead (Mile 54.4)
Proceed north of the Pactola Visitor Center, following US 385 to about the middle of the dam. Take a hard right onto the Pactola Basin Road, which begins on top of the dam. The trailhead is located at the base of the dam.

Tamarack Gulch Trailhead (Mile 54.9)
Use the same directions as for Rapid Creek Trailhead, but proceed 0.5 mile farther along the Basin Dam Road. Signs point to the respective trailheads.

Brush Creek Trailhead (Mile 59.4)
From US 385 turn east onto Forest Road 159, which you must follow for 2.6 miles down a dirt road to the trailhead. Proceeding south, the trail climbs several hills and descends 5 miles later on Dakota Point, located on Sheridan Lake.

Dakota Point Trailhead (Mile 64.4)

From Hill City follow US 385 north past Sheridan Lake to the Sheridan Lake Road. Proceed 1 mile to the trailhead.

Spring Creek Trailhead (Mile 64.6)

The route is about the same as the previous trailhead, though Spring Creek provides a 0.2-mile spur access.

Flume Trailhead (Mile 66.1)

This trailhead is located adjacent to the Sheridan Lake Campground. Follow the signs to the South Marina. At 1 mile from this trailhead, the Flume Trail crisscrosses the Centennial Trail. Hikers then have the option of proceeding farther along the Flume Trail or proceeding either north or south along the Centennial Trail proper.

Samelius Trailhead (Mile 71.1)

This trailhead is located just north of U.S. Highway 16. Hikers from this point will quickly proceed through a tunnel, which passes under US 16. Three miles later the trail links with the Big Pine Trailhead, described in subsequent paragraphs.

Willow Creek Trailhead and Horse Camp (Mile 73.1)

This trailhead provides a 4-mile spur to the Centennial Trail, which departs from near the KOA Campground along South Dakota Highway 244.

Big Pine Trailhead (Mile 74.1)

The 8.3-mile stretch between Big Pine and Iron Creek trailheads begins on the north side of SD 244 (about 3 miles west of Mount Rushmore), where it progresses south. Within a mile, the trail passes a spur linking with the Willow Creek Trailhead. From here, the trail ascends steeply, passing Elkhorn Mountain, and enters the Black Elk Wilderness Area, periodically offering views of Harney Peak.

About 4 miles from the trailhead, this segment of the Centennial Trail passes just west of Mount Rushmore National Monument. It continues its general downward progression for about 5 miles to the Iron Creek Trailhead, located on the border with Custer State Park.

Iron Creek Trailhead (Mile 82.4)

From the Peter Norbeck Visitor Center in Custer State Park, follow US 16A west for 5.2 miles until the road intersects with South Dakota Highway 87N. Follow SD 87 north for 5.7 miles to the sign for the trailhead. Follow the dirt road for 0.1 mile to the trailhead sign. The Centennial Trail is located between the sign and exit from the dirt road back to SD 87.

In Custer the trail follows a progression of beaver dams, then departs the stream where it assumes an easy up-and-down progression, passing over a series of small hills.

◀ *French Creek has sinkholes in spots, creating "now u see 'em, now u don't" areas.*

Badger Hole Trailhead (Mile 89.7)

From the Peter Norbeck Visitor Center, take US 16A west for 5.5 miles to the turnoff on the left for the Badger Hole. Proceed 1 mile to the trailhead, which links to the short road to the Charles Badger Clark Memorial (Badger Clark Historic Trail).

This 4.2-mile continuation of the Centennial Trail begins by swinging around a local treatment plant. The trail then ascends into a burn area, interesting as it provides a bird's-eye view of plant succession following a fire. The trail progresses over rolling landscape, mixed with ponderosa and prairie grass. Wildlife, including bison, abound.

French Creek Horse Camp Trailhead (Mile 93.9)

To access the trailhead, head east from Peter Norbeck Visitor Center on US 16A. Go 0.8 mile to the Wildlife Loop Road, on the right. Turn right and follow this road south for 20 miles to Blue Bell Lodge. From here, take Custer State Park Road 4 (gravel) east for 3 miles to the trailhead.

Highland Creek Trailhead (Mile 104.2)

This trailhead is accessed most easily from NPS Park Road 5 located in the northern portion of Wind Cave National Park. The dirt road must be followed for about 2 miles before reaching this access point.

This 6.2-mile segment departs from a prairie setting and wanders through stands of ponderosa pine (see Highland Creek–Centennial Loop Trail). It provides the possibility of encounters with bison, prairie dogs, elk, and pronghorn antelope. It offers periodic views of Rankin Ridge Lookout and glimpses of a dynamic prairie ecosystem as well.

Norbeck Lake Trailhead (Mile 110.4)

Depending on your route, this trailhead will be either the beginning or the end of your Centennial Trail hike. Or it might represent the start and finish of a day outing. Either way, you are in for some exciting times. As you hike this long trail, you'll get wonderful views of mountains, prairies, and wildlife. You'll find seclusion; you'll wade creeks; you might even get caught in a thunderstorm.

Access this trailhead from near the Wind Cave Visitor Center. Follow US 385 north for about 1 mile, then take the right turn near the prairie-dog town for SD 87, which you must then follow north for 1.5 miles. The trailhead is on your right.

56 George S. Mickelson Trail

According to its namesake and founder, George S. Mickelson, "This trail may be our last opportunity to provide a pathway that is easily used by the elderly, people with disabilities and the very young, as well as hikers, bicyclists and other more traditional trail users." Begun in 1991, the Mickelson Trail now represents the completion of the dream of a 114-mile-long trail traversing the beautiful Black Hills.

The concept was conceived in part by South Dakota governor George Mickelson, who intended that a trail should pass through the heart of the Black Hills. Mickelson envisioned a trail that would follow the historic Burlington Northern Railroad from Deadwood to Edgemont, which was abandoned from 1983 to 1989. In response to the abandonment, a group of local citizens decided to preserve the rail-line corridor and develop a recreation trail.

Mickelson remained a strong advocate of the trail, but was unable to see his vision completed. Following his untimely death in 1993, the trail was named in his honor.

This trail, with fourteen trailheads along an old rail bed, offers glimpses into the history of the Black Hills. From it you'll see old gold camps, claim cabins, cliff cuts, hard-rock tunnels, over one hundred converted bridges, high trestles, and pristine streams, as well as more modern creations such as the Crazy Horse Memorial. In many places the old rail bed is remote enough to offer a backcountry experience. The trail grade is not greater than 4 percent. To further enhance your enjoyment and add a greater dimension to your trip, thirty interpretive panels are found along the length of the trail.

The trail is open to mountain bikers, skiers, horseback riders, and those on foot. No motorized vehicles are allowed, except for a portion between Deadwood and Dumont. Bikers must yield to walkers, and all must yield to horses. The trail is closed from dusk to dawn, and camping is prohibited on the trail right-of-way and at the trailheads. Pets must be on leashes. You'll find parking, toilets, and self-sale passes at all of the trailheads. Picnic shelters exist along the trail; one such shelter is at the Hill City trailhead, honoring the Burlington Northern rail line.

To help maintain the trail, users age twelve and older are required to pay a $2.00 per day or a $10.00 per season user fee. Those using the trail within the city limits of towns along the way are not charged a fee. Passes are available at stations along the trail and at some state park offices. For information, contact the Black Hills Trail Office, HC 37, Box 604, Lead, SD 57754 (605–584–3896), or the Department of Game, Fish and Parks, 523 East Capitol, Pierre, SD 57501 (605–773–3391). The Web site is at www.mickelsontrail.com.

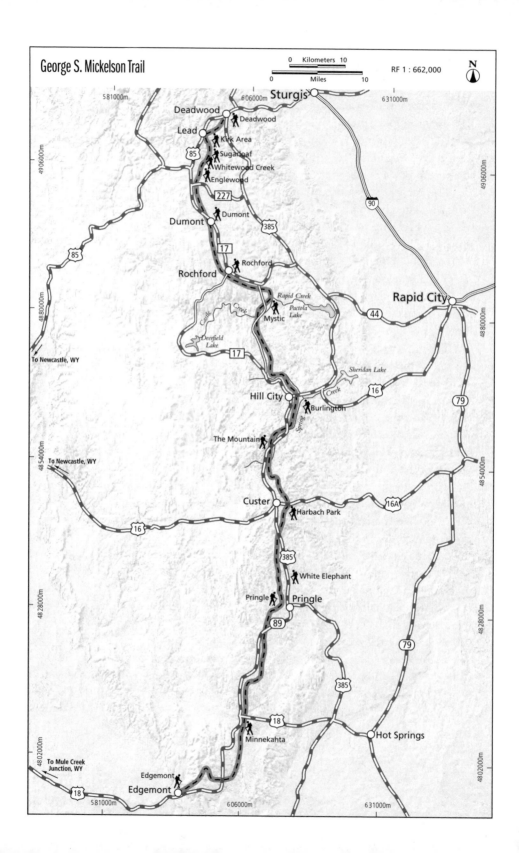

The Mickelson Trail approaches the evolving Crazy Horse Memorial.

The segment from Deadwood to Dumont offers five trailheads. If one proceeds north to south as we did, the trail is generally uphill, passing through forests and skirting some private farmland.

The following are meant to offer a sampling of this beautiful trail.

Deadwood and Kirk Trailheads

The trail leaves the town of Deadwood, then skirts the town of Lead and climbs until it overlooks Lead and the various mining operations of the Homestake Mining Company. After departing Lead, the trail passes through remote areas of timber alternating with farms and meadows. In places the trail is steep, though it levels near the Englewood Trailhead.

Locate the Deadwood Trailhead in Deadwood on U.S. Highway 85 at Deadwood Gulch Lodge, and find the Kirk Trailhead just south of Lead.

Sugarloaf Trailhead

Access this trailhead just 2 miles south of Lead on US 85.

The Mickelson Trail provides access to the area's mining history as well as to a variety of natural features.

Whitewood Creek, Englewood, and Dumont Trailheads

Follow U.S. Highway 385 for 8 miles south to its junction at Brownsville with Forest Road 227 (just across from Nemo Road). Follow this road west for 5 miles until it intersects with Forest Road 205. Whitewood Creek Trailhead is 3.5 miles north of this intersection; Englewood Trailhead is 1 mile farther. The Dumont Trailhead is on FR 205 just 3 miles south of its intersection with FR 227 or 8.7 miles north of Rochford.

Another segment of the Mickelson Trail passes from Hill City to Custer and then goes on to Pringle and Edgemont, where the Mickelson Trail ends. A convenient access point for the trail in Hill City is near the Tracy City Park in Hill City. The trail proceeds along a level course for several miles before it climbs and scurries over the pass near the Crazy Horse Memorial.

From here the trail proceeds downhill to the Custer Trailhead, located in Harbach City Park in the town of Custer. The trail then climbs slightly but generally maintains a level course to its junction with the Pringle Trailhead 14 miles later. This segment of the trail parallels Beaver Creek, which in places is a particularly beautiful waterway.

Appendix A: Suggested Equipment

Even the most experienced hiker is sometimes well into a hike when he or she remembers a forgotten but necessary item. The following list is intended to help in preventing such occurrences, ensuring a more enjoyable trip. Some items on the list are essentials, but others can be included according to personal preference. Always keep the weight factor in mind—unless you can pack as much as a llama or a horse.

Weather in the Black Hills can be fickle. Thundershowers come on a regular basis in the summer months. And if you're high on a mountain trail during a sudden shower, it can suddenly get very cold. So even if it's seventy-five degrees at your campsite, carry enough warm clothes and good rain gear to be prepared. Hiking boots should be of good quality and already broken in. Many a trip has been ruined in the first few hours by new or poorly fitting boots. If you've purchased something new for a hike (tent, backpack, boots, etc.), it's a good idea to try it out, break it in, or set it up before embarking on your trek.

One final caution about drinking the water. Don't. Don't drink it until it has been purified with an acceptable system, that is. Wind Cave National Park and Badlands National Park have little water, and both these places are hot and dry in the summer. The advice of most rangers in the Black Hills is to pack your own water. Take the water weight factor into account when planning a hike of any length.

The following checklists will help you pack well for any day or backpack trip in the Black Hills:

Clothing

___good-quality rain gear

___warm jacket

___Windbreaker

___wind pants

___long underwear

___long pants

___lightweight long-sleeve shirt(s)

___T-shirts and shorts

___sweater or heavy shirt

___socks for each day plus one set extra

___underwear

___hats, one wool, one with sun visor

___gloves

___belt

___good hiking boots

___extra shoes or sandals for camp and stream crossings

Food

___hot- and cold-drink mixes (tea, coffee)

___dry food (dry your own or buy commercial meals, rice, beans, noodles)

___hot cereal to mix with water

___trail mix (make your own)

___high-energy snacks

Hiking equipment

___tent and rain fly

___warm sleeping bag and pad with stuff sacks

___full-size backpack

___day pack for shorter side trips from a base camp

___backpack stove and fuel

___cooking pot

___cup

___bowl

___utensils

___water bottle

___waterproof matches in container

Miscellaneous

___compass

___maps

___tick and insect repellent

___sunscreen and lipscreen

___sunglasses

___toilet paper

___toothbrush

___biodegradable soap

___small towel/washcloth

___small backpack shovel

___garbage sack

___plastic sandwich bags

___pocket knife

___binoculars

___water filter or purification tablets

___first-aid kit

___flashlight and batteries

___camera and film

___fishing gear and license
___pocket notebook and pencil
___50-foot length of nylon cord
___waterproof backpack cover
___paperback book

Appendix B: Managing Agencies

The following agencies are excellent sources for maps, hiking and camping information, and reservations, books, and other materials concerning the Black Hills.

USDA Forest Service

Bearlodge Ranger District
U.S. Highway 14 East, Box 680
Sundance, WY 82729
(307) 283–1361

Hell Canyon Ranger District
Newcastle Office
1225 Washington Boulevard
Newcastle, WY 82701
(307) 746–2783

Custer Office
330 Mount Rushmore Road
Custer, SD 57730
(605) 673–4853

Mystic Ranger District
Harney Office
23939 U.S. Highway 385
Hill City, SD 57745
(605) 574–2534

Mystic Office
803 Soo San Drive
Rapid City, SD 57702
(605) 343–1567

Black Hills National Forest
Visitor Center
23939 U.S. Highway 385
Hill City, SD 57745
(605) 574–2534

Northern Hills Ranger District
2014 North Main
Spearfish, SD 57783
(605) 642–4622

**Black Hills National Forest
Supervisor's Office and
Visitor Center**
RR 2, Box 200
Custer, SD 57730
(605) 673–2251

Bear Butte State Park
P.O. Box 688
Sturgis, SD 57785
(605) 347–5240

**Black Hills Parks and Forest
Association**
26611 U.S. Highway 385
Hot Springs, SD 57747
(605) 745–4600

Bureau of Land Management
310 Roundup
Belle Fourche, SD 57717
(605) 892–2526

Bureau of Land Management
1225 Washington Boulevard
Newcastle, WY 82701
(307) 746–4453

Custer State Park
HC 83, Box 70
Custer, SD 57730
(605) 255–4515

Devils Tower National Monument
P.O. Box 8
Devils Tower, WY 82714
(307) 467–5283

Mount Rushmore National Memorial
P.O. Box 268
Keystone, SD 57751
(605) 574–2523

South Dakota Department of Tourism
711 East Wells Avenue
Pierre, SD 57501-3369
(800) 732–5682

Wind Cave National Park
RR 1, Box 190
Hot Springs, SD 57747
(605) 745–4600

Wyoming Division of Tourism
I–25 at College Drive
Cheyenne, WY 82002
(800) 225–5996

Appendix C: Campgrounds and Maps

Campgrounds

Campgrounds are abundant in the Black Hills, ranging from those with facilities to ones that are primitive and not so easily accessible. There is something for everyone. Some require reservations, so it's a good idea to call ahead, especially for the busier summer months. For those unable to plan ahead, keep in mind that, as a general rule, the unreserved sites become available early in the morning as other campers pull out. Campgrounds on or near lakes and those offering shower facilities seem to fill the fastest.

Backcountry or wilderness camping is allowed in most of the Black Hills and Badlands National Park. Some areas require a backcountry camping permit, and all areas have certain regulations, which can be obtained from the visitor centers or ranger stations. Practice zero-impact camping wherever you go.

Badlands National Park

Two campgrounds. Cedar Pass Campground is located near the Ben Reifel Visitor Center and has water and restrooms. Winter camping is free here. Sage Creek Primitive Campground is in the Sage Creek Wilderness Area; it has no water, and campfires are not permitted.

Bearlodge Mountains

Three campgrounds in the vicinity of the Black Hills trails: Cook Lake, Reuter Campground, and Sundance Campground.

Black Hills National Forest

Twenty-eight campgrounds; all but three have drinking water from spring to fall. To reserve, call (800) 280–2267.

Custer State Park

Seven campgrounds with individual sites (and water and showers). Some are reserved, some are first-come, first-served sites. Call (800) 710–2267 for reservations. Additionally, there are two primitive camping sites in the French Creek Natural Area.

Wind Cave

One campground, Elk Mountain, located 1 mile from the visitor center. Water and restrooms from spring through fall.

Maps

Several types of maps are available for the Black Hills hiker and can be obtained at the visitor centers, the agency offices, and sporting-goods stores throughout the area. Maps may also be obtained by writing or calling the agencies. Many are free, others are available for purchase. The free maps, descriptive booklets, and trail guides offered by the Forest Service, Custer State Park, Wind Cave National Park, and Badlands National Park serve as excellent guides.

Providing completely accurate mileages of trails is difficult, and hikers should bear in mind that the trails may be slightly shorter or longer than indicated. Additionally, sometimes the trail lengths differ on the maps from what is posted on the trail signs. More important than the actual length, though, is often the difficulty rating. A very strenuous trail of 2 miles often seems and takes longer than an easy one of 5 miles.

The Black Hills National Forest Map, $3.00, with a scale of 2 miles to the inch, is available at visitor centers and USDA Forest Service offices.

Quad and topographical maps may be obtained for a fee from visitor centers and USDA Forest Service offices, as well as from the following:

National Geographic/Trails Illustrated
P.O. Box 4357
Evergreen, CO 80437-4357
(303) 670-3457
(800) 962-1643

Maps available:
Black Hills South, No. 238
Black Hills Northeast, No. 751
Badlands National Park, SD No. 239

U.S. Geological Survey National Mapping Division
12201 Sunrise Valley Drive
Mail Stop 809
Reston, VA 22092
(703) 648-7070

Branch of Distribution
USGS Federal Center
Denver, CO 80225

Appendix D: Selected Reading

Many of the following books were helpful resources as we prepared this book. Others make fascinating reading. The Natural History Association of the Black Hills has available a wonderful selection of books for all ages. The visitor centers within the Black Hills also have a great inventory of books for sale. Topics available in both places include natural history, history, Native American history and lore, hiking advice, children's books and coloring books. The list is extensive.

Dodge, Richard Irving. *The Black Hills.* 1876.

Fletcher, Colin. *The Complete Walker III.* New York: Alfred A. Knopf, 1974.

Froiland, Sven G. *Natural History of the Black Hills and Badlands.* Sioux Falls, S. Dak.: Augustana College Center for Western Studies, 1990.

Grubbs, Bruce. *Using GPS.* Helena, Mont.: Falcon Publishing, Inc., 1999.

Harmon, Will. *Wild Country Companion.* Helena, Mont.: Falcon Publishing, Inc., 1994.

Moeller, Bill, and Jan Moeller. *Crazy Horse, His Life, His Lands: A Photographic Biography.* Woodburn, Ore.: Beautiful America Publishing Co., 1987.

A Practical Guide to Outdoor Protection. Sawyer Products, 1994.

Raventon, Edward. *Island in the Plains, A Black Hills Natural History.* Boulder, Colo.: Johnson Printing Company, 1994.

Sandoz, Mari. *Crazy Horse, Strange Man of the Oglalas.* Lincoln, Neb.: University of Nebraska Press, 1942.

Turchen, Lesta Van Der Wert. *The Black Hills Expedition of 1875.* 1975.

Van Bruggen, Theodore. *Wildflowers, Grasses, and Other Plants of the Northern Plains and Black Hills.* Interior, S. Dak.: Badlands Natural History Association, 1992.

The following titles are a small sampling of those that may be ordered from the Black Hills Parks & Forests Association, 26611 U.S. Highway 385, Hot Springs, SD 57747:

Birdwatcher's Guide to the Black Hills
Crazy Horse
Custer State Park Grasslands
Devils Tower
Where the Buffalo Roam
Wind Cave–An Ancient World Beneath the Hills

About the Authors

Bert and Jane Gildart are self-described "wanderers," seeking out special places across the country. Together they have hiked, biked, skied, and boated hundreds of miles throughout many wilderness and backcountry areas, in addition to exploring our national parks.

For thirteen summers Bert served as a backcountry ranger in Glacier National Park. He is the author of more than 400 magazine articles and eleven books.

Bert and Jane have collaborated on several FalconGuides including: *Hiking Shenandoah National Park; Best Easy Day Hikes Shenandoah National Park; A FalconGuide to Dinosaur National Monument;* and *A FalconGuide to Death Valley National Park.* When not off wandering, they make their home in northwest Montana, in the shadow of Glacier National Park.

The authors, Jane and Bert Gildart.